To ~~Susan K~~

With much love —

Dan E. Perry

12/10/08   *Rom 1:16*

THE GAME
OF LIFE

... and How to Play It

The writing of this book was given to me by the grace of God. It is now my privilege to pass it on to you as a gift, free of any charge or obligation. It would, however, give me great pleasure for you to make a donation of any amount to one of the following three worthy causes:

- Faith Fellowship Church (for: the Building fund)
  2278 Paul's Path Road, Kinston, NC 28504
- The Salvation Army (for: use in Kinston, NC)
  P.O. Box 1479, Kinston, NC 28503-1479
- Son Set Ministries (for: the Refuge)
  P.O. Box 5247, Kinston, NC 28503-5247

I pray that, as you read this book, you will discover the "game of life" and how to play it.

Dan E. Perry, Attorney
P.O. Box 1475 | Kinston, NC 28503-1475

THE GAME OF LIFE

OF LIFE

...and How to Play It

DAN E. PERRY

CHAPEL HILL
PRESS, INC.

This book is dedicated to my dear wife

Margaret

who has been my sweetheart
and best friend for over forty-five years.
Through God's grace and mercy,
He has given me both
the right and privilege of
playing the game of life.
As an extra bonus He gave me
Margaret as my loving helpmate
and companion and the mother of
our three children, so as to make
the game both exciting and rewarding.

Contents

ACKNOWLEDGMENTS ix

PREFACE   Relating to the Game of Life xi

INTRODUCTION xiii

Part One

CHAPTER 1   The World Offers Us Many Choices,
Eternity Only Two 3

CHAPTER 2   How to Begin Playing the Game of Life 7

CHAPTER 3   The College of Life 11

CHAPTER 4   Getting to Know Our Coach 17

CHAPTER 5   The Necessity of Preparation,
Training, and Discipline 23

CHAPTER 6   The Adversary Coach 33

Part Two

CHAPTER 7   Play Ball! Let the Game Begin! 39

CHAPTER 8   Learning from Our Adversities 65

CHAPTER 9   Observations Made from My Playing
the Game of Life 75

CHAPTER 10   A Review: Seeing the Big Picture,
Summing Up the Game of Life, and
Passing It On to Others 85

CHAPTER 11   The Final Chapter—Mission Accomplished:
Graduation from the College of Life 91

CHAPTER 12   The Degree of Doctor of Philosophy in
Homemaking Is Awarded to Elizabeth Ann
Seipp Perry from the College of Life 101

CHAPTER 13   A Time to Reflect and Decide. 107

POSTLUDE   111
HOME AT LAST   115
CONCLUDING NOTE TO THE READER 119

Acknowledgments

I am thankful for my wife, Margaret, not only for her input and thoughts, but also for her encouragement and patience in putting up with me during the writing of this book.

Because of their belief in the inerrancy of God's Word, I asked my friends Jason McKnight, Barbara Ruth Perry, and Randy Spaugh to review and critique the manuscript before publication. Each gave me several suggestions that I incorporated in the final product. For their gift of time and effort I am most grateful.

A special thanks to my typist, Linda Murray, for her usual fine job in working tirelessly with me in putting it all together.

Thanks also to Edwina Woodbury and Dennis McGill of the Chapel Hill Press as well as to graphic designer Katie Severa for their expertise, encouragement, and patience. Each of them has been invaluable in the publication of this book.

Preface

RELATING TO THE GAME OF LIFE

Soon after my first book, *More Than I Deserve*, was published, I began thinking about this second book. My purpose and intention here are to relate or compare my journey through this life to an athletic contest such as football or basketball. All such games have certain rules, and the game of life is no exception. In learning to play any game, the first question is, what are the rules and how do you play it? But there are many other similarities. The same can be said about the game of life. If I were a star high school basketball player and heavily recruited by various colleges (which I wasn't), I would first want to know the name and reputation of the school, and what conference it's in. Is it in the highly respected ACC, or some minor, little-known conference? Who's the recruiter? Who's the coach? What are his credentials? If it's Roy Williams of UNC, that's one thing, but if it's John Jones of Podunk College, that's another. What kind of reputation does he have for winning? Accordingly, if I go to the "College of Life" to play the game of life, similar questions can be asked: Who's the coach? What are the perks, and can I get a scholarship? Will it be a rewarding experience? What kind of facilities does the school provide? Can the coach teach me to be a better player? What about my future?

My hope is that, as the reader proceeds, he will see the unfolding of a meaningful relationship between a sporting event and the "game of life".

Introduction

I've always enjoyed games—all sorts of games. Some of my earliest memories include the childhood party games of ring-around-the-roses, pin the tail (on the donkey), and kick the can. In grammar school it was dodgeball and kickball. Then there were football, baseball, basketball, and golf. Other games were checkers, Chinese checkers, and various card games such as gin rummy and hearts. One of my favorite board games was Monopoly. The list goes on and on.

I enjoyed playing most of the games, but some I didn't like for various reasons. Chess and bridge were just too complicated and time consuming. Soon after Margaret and I were married, my sister-in-law, Barbara Ruth, invited us to join a couple's bridge club. I knew very little if anything about the game, but it was the thing to do (because everybody was doing it), so we gave it a try. I think we lasted only two or three sessions. Neither of us liked it. For us the answer was easy. We didn't enjoy it, so we chose to quit. Bridge was simply not our cup of tea. We didn't want to play, so we didn't. Why should we keep on playing a game we didn't like?

That's the way it is with any game in our society. If we don't like it, we don't play it. Nobody is going to force us to play a game we choose not to play. But wait, there's an obvious exception! There's one game we all *must* play whether we like it or not—and that is the game of life. In that game we don't have a choice. From the time we are born and begin to develop our senses, we begin playing this game of life. In beginning his speech at the Jaycees Distinguished Service Award Banquet in Kinston about 1960, I heard Norman Vincent Peale say, "We're all in the business of living!" He went on to say whether we like it or not we all must live, day after day, year after year—until we die! Dr. Peale called it "the business of living." I'm going to call it "the game of life."

A Note to the Discerning Reader

If I had written this book right after hearing Dr. Peale, I would have thought that the business of living and the game of life were basically one and the same. After all, both topics seem to refer to the living out of our lives on a daily basis until we die. But the truth is that there is a distinct difference. In the spring of 1987 at the age of fifty-six when I started the serious study of God's Word, I began to realize that in the spiritual world there are not just one but two games, and only two games, available to each of us. The "game of life" is one, and by far the most rewarding. The only other game we can play during our lifetime is called the "game of death." The foundation and basic concept of this book deal with defining, explaining, and contrasting these two games.

For those who read my first book, *More Than I Deserve*, if you detect the repetition of some of the truths and lessons I've learned along my journey through life, there's a good reason for it. It's because I feel their importance cannot be overly emphasized. Things of eternal value deserve to be repeated for their far-reaching significance in the life of the reader. My overall purpose is to draw the reader to Jesus Christ, to see the need to accept Him as Lord and Savior—and to grow and mature in a daily relationship with Him.

PART ONE

Understanding the Game of Life

Chapter 1

THE WORLD OFFERS US MANY CHOICES, ETERNITY ONLY TWO

You've got to be in the right arena. It's a matter of life or death!

During our earthly existence we all live in two different worlds: the physical world and the spiritual world. In the physical world, we have literally thousands of various types of games from which to choose—whether they're athletic games, card games, or board games. In America we have been given the freedom to play any of these games we want, as many times as we want, or we can choose not to play any of them at all. It's up to our own individual liking. Nobody is going to force us to play a particular game against our will.

In the spiritual world the rules and choices are entirely different. We have only two games from which to choose. As odd as it may seem, the spiritual Rule Book forces us to play one or the other. Each individual must decide for him or herself. This holds true no matter what our race, color, creed, or nationality, whether Jew, Gentile, Buddhist, or Muslim. Simply put, it's a matter of life or death, for one is known as the game of life and the other is the game of death.

The Game of Death

Whether we like it or not, we all start our earthly existence playing the game of death. We don't have a choice. The minute we are born, the ball game begins. It all started in the Garden of Eden with the sin of disobedience of Adam and Eve. After that, every person born in the world inherited their sinful nature and will continue to be plagued by it for the rest of their earthly existence. We will continue playing this game of death until such time as we choose to stop by surrendering to God's call. The only way to stop playing the game of death is to choose to play the alternative game—the game of life. Remember, we can't play both at the same time. We must play one or the other. It's either death or life!

The two major problems with playing the game of death throughout our earthly existence are, first, we are deceived into thinking we are "happy" while playing it. The truth is, whatever "happiness" we may find is only temporary; it has no lasting value. Second, it doesn't stop when our earthly existence is over. It continues on throughout all eternity, which the Rule Book (known as the Bible) calls the "second death." This is an eternal existence separated from the Creator and Author of the Rule Book. In modern language we call Him the Sovereign God of the Universe. He called this second death (to put it mildly) a place of separation and darkness where there will be "weeping and gnashing of teeth." We have the assurance of the Author that no one would deliberately choose to go there, and yet, that's exactly where we will be unless something is done during our earthly existence. The answer—and the only answer? To choose to play the game of life, which the Rule Book calls eternal life.

The Game of Life

The Sovereign God of the universe, who is the Author, Founder, and "Inventor" of the game of life, created us all with fellowship in mind. In Genesis 1:26 of the Rule Book, the Author inspired Moses to write, "Let us make man in our image, according to our likeness." In saying, "Let us," He is referring to the Father, the Son (Jesus), and the Holy Spirit, who might be called the Co-Authors of the game of life (see John 1). A closer look at the context of the entire passage leads us to conclude what Charles Stanley calls Life Principle #1. In essence it says that God's highest priority for our lives is that we have an intimate relationship with Him, the three Co-Authors of the game (also known as the Godhead). It's important to understand that the degree of our intimacy with God determines the impact of our lives and how well we play the game of life. God wants the best for all of the players on His team. When we fully experience and respond to His love for us as players, we can better and more fully love one another. That love relationship among the players is essential to creating a winning team. It goes without saying that all of us want to be on the winning team; and it is only through that intimate relationship with God that we can be inspired to win the game of life.

> **Insight:** The game plan for winning in the game of life is to put our trust in the Author and giver of life and the second person of the Godhead. Jesus said, "I am the way, the truth and the life; no one comes to the Father except through me" (John 14:6). What He's saying is that we can't even begin playing the game of life without trusting in Jesus.

Chapter 2

HOW TO BEGIN PLAYING THE GAME OF LIFE

First things first. You must be born again! That's God's design.

To fully understand the number-one requirement for how to begin to play the game of life, it is essential that we have a firm grasp of the nature of our earthly existence. We must all understand that at birth we not only have a physical body, but there is also a spiritual part of all believers that will be given a spiritual body at the second coming of Jesus. At our physical birth our body is alive, but our spirit is dead. In order to begin playing the game of life our dead spirit must be regenerated and made alive. The skeptics would question, how could that be? That is impossible! How can my dead spirit be made alive?

A Seeker Searches for the Answer

The Author of the Rule Book gives the answer as revealed in a conversation recorded in the *third chapter of the Gospel of John*. A learned and pious leader of the Jews by the name of Nicodemus secretively came to Jesus at night. He had closely observed Jesus as being someone special and said, "for no one can do these signs (miracles) unless God is with him." Jesus (being the Co-Author of the game of life) knew his innermost thoughts and perceived that Nicodemas was really asking the age-old question, "What must I do to have eternal life?" Jesus' answer was right to the point: "Most assuredly, I say to you, unless one is born again he cannot see the Kingdom of God." Nicodemus lacked spiritual insight and was confused by Jesus' answer, for he had no understanding of the fact that he was not only a physical being but also a spiritual being. Jesus explained the difference by saying, "That which is born of the flesh is flesh and that which is born of the spirit is spirit. Do not marvel that I said to you, 'You must be born again.'"

And that's what you and I must do if we want to be a member of the winning team. We must be born again. Our spirit must be regenerated or made alive. If we are to play the game of life we must be spiritually alive; otherwise we are destined to continue playing that dreadful game of death.

What Does It Mean to Be Born Again?

To be born again requires faith and not works. The Bible says, "But without faith it is impossible to please Him, for he who comes to God must believe that He is, and that He is a rewarder of those who diligently seek Him" (Hebrews 11:6). It also says, "For by grace you have been saved through faith, and not of yourselves, it is the gift of God, not of works, least anyone should boast" (Ephesians 2:8–9). God's grace is activated when we receive something we don't deserve. We don't deserve to be saved from our sins, but He offers us salvation anyway because of His amazing unconditional love.

When we are born again we are saved from our sins. Sin is what separates us from God and keeps us from having eternal life with Him. Sin can be loosely defined as "anything we do that puts our wishes or agenda above God's"—in other words, anything that puts me in God's place. The first of the Ten Commandments says, "You shall have no other gods before me" (Exodus 20:3). God is holy and sinless in all respects, and if we are to live eternally with Him after we leave this earthly existence we too must be holy and without sin. Our whole objective is to have peace with God and to live in His eternal presence.

The following Scriptures will help us see that God loves us and wants us to experience peace and life—abundant life while on earth and eternal life after our earthly existence is over:

- "We have peace with God through our Lord Jesus Christ" (Romans 5:1).
- "For God so loved the world that he gave His only begotten Son, that whosoever believes in Him shall not perish but have eternal life" (John 3:16).
- "I (Jesus) have come that they may have life, and that they may have it more abundantly" (John 10:10).

We Have Two Major Problems

1. Our first major problem is that we are separated from God. God originally created man in His own image to have an abundant life. He did not make him a robot to automatically love and obey Him. He gave him a will and freedom of choice. Mankind chose to disobey God and go his own willful way. He still makes that choice today. This is old-fashioned sin and results in our being separated from God.

2. Our second major problem is that most of us don't even realize we have this problem of separation. We don't think we need a relationship with God. We think we can make it on our own. We believe we can go through life independent of the God who made us.

The Bible says we are all sinners—every single one of us, without exception. "For all have sinned and fall short of the glory of God" (Romans 3:23). The Bible also says that sin leads to death: "For the wages of sin is death, but the gift of God is eternal life in Christ Jesus our Lord" (Romans 6:23).

Can We Bridge the Gap?

People have tried in countless ways to bridge the gap between themselves and God—through good works, religion, philosophy, morality, and all sorts of good and honorable things as well as other gods. The world system says that if you work hard enough and do enough good works, you can earn your way to heaven. Such ways may give the appearance of the right way, but they all lead to a dead end, The Bible says, "There is a way that seems right to a man, but in the end it leads to death" (Proverbs 14:12). Through the ages men have thought that they could come to God in their own way, by their own strength, but all such foolish attempts have been and will always be futile. The Bible points out the error of their ways by saying, "Professing to be wise, they became fools" (Romans 1:22).

God Sees Our Need and Gives Us the Answer

God has provided a way to bridge the gap between us as a sinful people and Him as a holy God. It is God's way, and according to His design from before the foundation of the world, it is the only way. All other attempts have failed in the past, and will continue to fail according to God's holy Word. What is the only way? It is through His Son, Jesus the Christ, who died on the cross and rose from the grave. He paid our sin debt in full. He paid the penalty for our sin and bridged the gap between us and God.

The Bible says, "For there is one God and one mediator between God and man, the man Jesus Christ" (Timothy 2:5). It also says, "For Christ died for sins once for all, the righteous for the unrighteous, to bring you to God" (1 Peter 3:18). As a further explanation, Romans 5:8 says, "But God demonstrated his own love for us in this: while we were still sinners, Christ died for us."

Our Response: Receive Christ

In response to God's unconditional love for all mankind, we need to trust Jesus Christ as Lord and Savior and receive Him by God's personal invitation.

   The Bible says ...
   - "Here I am! I stand at the door and knock. If anyone hears my voice and opens the door, I will come in and eat with him, and he with me" (Revelation 3:20).
   - "Yet to all who receive Him, to those who believe in His name, He gave the right to become children of God" (John 1:12).
   - "That if you confess with your mouth, 'Jesus is Lord,' and believe in your heart that God raised Him from the dead, you will be saved" (Romans 10:9).

Chapter 3

THE COLLEGE OF LIFE

*Now that we decided to play the game of life,
we are ready to go to college.*

Why should we go to college? All great athletes seek to play in the big leagues and be trained by the top coaches. They want to take their skills to the next level—from high school to college. Two of the best basketball coaches in the country are right here in our state of North Carolina. Both Roy Williams of the North Carolina Tar Heels and Mike Krzyzewski of the Duke Blue Devils are part of long-winning traditions. They have surrounded themselves with a staff of the highest quality. As long as the players work as a team and follow their coach's instructions, they will eventually be winners, whether or not they actually win a conference or national championship.

The same is true of the College of Life. It also has a winning tradition. It has the top (and only) Coach in the business, and He is the one who sets the example and provides the foundation upon which to produce winners. He seeks out all those who are willing to come to His College and play the game of life according to His rules.

Recruiting the Players

Every great college team has at least one if not several top recruiters. Their job is to find the players who have the potential to play at their school and become champions. The College of Life has the three best coaches in the business. We call them the Father (known as God), the Son (known as Jesus), and the Holy Spirit (known as the Helper, the Comforter, and the Spirit of God). As a team of Coaches they are called the Trinity or Godhead because they work so closely together. In fact, Jesus said, "I and my Father are one" (John 10:30). He also said, "The Father is in me, and I in Him" (John 10:39). The Recruiter is the Holy Spirit, and it's His job not only to recruit but to help train those whom the Father chooses to go to the College of Life. No player can go to the College of Life unless he is chosen by the Father through the Son. John 15:19 says, "I [the Son, Jesus] chose you out of the world." According to John 6:44, "No one can come to Me [Jesus] unless the Father who sent Me draws him."

Passing the Entrance Exam

Once a player has been recruited to attend the College of Life, he must now pass the entrance exam. In other words, he must be born of the spirit, or as we have already explained, he must be born again. Different recruits take the exam in different ways, at different ages, and under different conditions. Some face difficult and trying times, which cause them to see the need for something more in their lives, which in reality is a Savior. It may be through some tragedy, sickness, or adverse circumstance whereby they see the Lord as a last resort. But for whatever reason, they must come by faith by putting their trust in Jesus as their Lord and Savior. That's the way the Creator and Founder designed it, and it is the only way you can gain entrance into the College of Life. It's really not a tough exam, for it is composed basically of only one question. Anyone who can answer that one question correctly, and sincerely mean what he or she says, can enter the College of Life. Actually, the Recruiter chooses the players, and therefore He will lead His chosen ones into passing the exam. So what's the big question?

My Own Personal Testimony

I had the privilege of passing the entrance exam to the College of Life at the age of twelve. The year was 1943, and we were at the Easter sunrise service at

Gordon Street Christian Church. The minister was Dr. J. Wayne Drash. I had been attending his pastor's class, which he had conducted for several of the church youth. We had reached the age where we could understand, at least to some degree, the meaning of having a relationship with the God of the Universe, and the Founder of the College of Life. I had been raised in a Christian family by a mother and father who loved and trained me, along with my two older brothers, by way of both precept and example. Mother and Daddy were both heavily involved in church and community-related activities as teachers and leaders. They always saw to it that we as a family were in Sunday school and church every Sunday. I shall be forever grateful for the nurturing and training I received at Gordon Street Christian Church, for it laid the foundation for my passing the entrance exam to the College of Life.

On Palm Sunday several of my friends came forward when Dr. Drash issued the invitation to accept Christ as Lord and Savior. I remember the feeling I had as the others made their way to the front of the church. In his pastor's class Dr. Drash had explained what it meant to accept Christ, but he also cautioned us that we were not to come forward just because "everybody else was doing it." We should wait until we felt that inward call upon our lives. As the others came forward I did not move. Somehow I was not ready. It was simply not my time. I clearly did not feel I should leave my seat. It was not until the following week at the sunrise service on Easter morning that I knew my time had come. The sermon was on the resurrection and the empty tomb. The invitation was given, and the closing hymn was being sung. I remember thinking, *Lord, I know my time has come. I know you want me to respond by going forward.* But for some reason I simply could not move; I guess I was just too scared. And then I reasoned, *If just one other person comes forward, I'll do it.* The Lord must have heard my plea, for within seconds, I saw a young soldier in uniform making his way to the front. It was during wartime, and we frequently had servicemen in the congregation. As I saw the young soldier shaking Dr. Drash's hand and softly whispering in his ear, I remember turning to Mother and Daddy and whispering something to the effect, "I'm going to get up." It was then I got up out of my pew seat and went forward to shake

Dr. Drash's hand and tell him I wanted to make my confession of faith. I was ready to answer the one question that would gain me entrance into the College of Life. After the closing hymn Dr. Drash seated the congregation and explained why the soldier and I were standing before them. After asking the question to the soldier and receiving his positive response he came to me.

The question was simple and direct. Dr. Drash asked me, **"Do you believe that Jesus is the Christ, the Son of the living God, and do you accept Him as your personal Lord and Savior?"** We were both looking at each other straight in the eyes as he shook my hand and asked me that all-important question. Without hesitation my answer came forth: **"I do!"** He then offered a word of congratulations and welcome, and following the benediction, the congregation also congratulated me. It was truly a red-letter day in my life. Several confirmed that it was "the most important decision you'll ever make!" At the time I didn't know the full impact my confession of faith would have on my life. The immediate effect was that I had a strong desire to read the Bible and find out more about God's Word and His plan for my life. Although I was only a novice and a mere freshman, the bottom line was that I was experiencing my first days in the College of Life, and the Head Coach was just starting the process of preparing me to play the game of life.

Putting It All in Perspective

A lot of colleges throughout the world make all sorts of promises and claims to all the gifted athletes, trying to entice them to attend their school. All such schools are based upon principles advancing what is known as the world system. They're in an entirely different category than the College of Life. Their promises sound good to the undiscerning and unsuspecting ear, but they all end with the same result. They lead to a continuation of the status quo.

Remember what we've already learned. There are only two colleges available in the spirit world: the College of Death and the College of Life. If you don't choose to attend the College of Life, you will, because of your sin nature inherited from Adam, remain forever in the College of Death. You may appear to win a lot of games during your College of Death career, but in reality those so-called victories are empty and fleeting. That may seem harsh and unloving, but it is the truth according to the Author of Life who designed the system from before the beginning of time. I will forever be grateful that I was recruited and answered the call by deciding to transfer from the College of Death to the College of Life. Although I was excited to have a new education ahead of me, I was never told it would be an easy road. The Coach did, however, assure me that if I was willing to read and abide by His rules as outlined in His Rule Book, He would provide the necessary inspiration and encouragement to see me through every tough game played. He further assured me I was already a winner! As someone said, "He didn't promise a smooth ride, but He did promise a safe landing."

Chapter 4

GETTING TO KNOW OUR COACH

*To get the most out of the game of life, we must know
our Coach and abide by His rules.*

Every great coach, no matter what the sport, requires strict discipline in following the rules of the game as well as the team rules laid down by the coach himself. The game of life is no different. As already explained in chapter 1, our Coach (being the Sovereign God of the Universe) is the Inventor and Author of the game of life. He knows every aspect of it. He made the rules, and He knows that if we follow His rules and depend on Him to play the game His way, we will live an abundant, victorious life. It will not always be easy, for there will be many aches and pains and injuries, along with disappointments and frustrations. But by the time we graduate He will have fulfilled His purpose through us according to His plan, because He is victorious, and in Him we are, too.

The Coach Knows His Players

After we have been born again and our spirit has become alive, we are now children of God. Many people are under the misconception that all human beings are children of God, but that is not according to His Word. The Bible says we become children of God only when we accept His Son as Lord and Savior. The Apostle John made this point clear when he wrote, "But as many as received Him He gave the right to become children of God, to those who believe in His name" (John 1:12). When we receive Jesus into our lives, we are receiving God's only begotten Son. In reality we then become God's sons or daughters by adoption. In other words, we have been adopted into the kingdom of God. In legal terms we have been adopted into the bloodstream of the adoptive parent. As adopted children of the sovereign God of the universe we are now entitled to the full inheritance of all the riches and blessings of His kingdom. What an inheritance that is! All of God's children have a lot to look forward to, both during our present earthly existence as well as in our future heavenly existence with our Father God.

As a child of God, He wants the very best for us—for all of His children. He has recruited us to go to the College of Life. We have responded by passing the entrance exam. Now He is ready to prepare us and mold us into the individual champion and team member He designed us to be—a winner in the game of life.

The Coach's Expectations and Overall Game Plan

The Coach knows His players, and He demands that the players know Him and abide by His rules. Let's look at four major expectations He has for all of His players:

1. *He Wants Us to Have an Intimate Relationship with Him.* This is His highest priority for us, and the degree of our intimacy with Him will determine the impact of our lives and our success as a player on His team. The key ingredient is love! Henry Drummond refers to love as "the greatest thing in the world," and our Coach goes so far as to say that I can have all the other gifts, talents, abilities, and riches the world has to offer, but unless I have love, "I am nothing" and "it profits me nothing" (1 Corinthians 13). He wants us to truly love and obey Him, and if we do, He will lead us to love others. His Rule Book says:
   - "We love Him because He first loved us" (1 John 4:19).
   - "He who loves God must love his brother also" (1 John 5:2).
   - "By this we know that we are the children of God, we love God and keep His Commandments" (1 John 5:2).

In order for us to experience God's love we must willingly surrender to His call to be our Coach, or as the Bible says, to be our Savior, Lord, and Friend. In his *Life Principle Bible*, Charles Stanley lists three reasons why God seeks our surrender:

a. He loves us and desires our fellowship and worship.

b. He wants our service for Him to be effective and fruitful. The more we get to know and love Jesus, the more effective our service will be. The closer we draw to God, the more impact our lives will have. The more energetically we nurture our relationship with the Lord, the greater the positive mark we will leave behind.

c. He waits for the freedom to bless us and make us better players in the game of life. God is our all-powerful and all-knowing Coach, and He draws us to Himself so we can experience His love and forgiveness. He wants us to willingly surrender our talents and lives to Him so He can give us the best blessings He has to offer. By surrendering to the Coach's will, He can teach us all we need to know to be the best players we can be on His team.

To repeat, our Coach's first desire and expectation of all His players is that we have an intimate relationship with Him.

2. *He Wants Us to Obey Him as Our Coach and Leave All the Consequences to Him.* Obeying the Coach is essential to pleasing Him. He knows what's best for us as players and for us as a team. He gives us principles to live by and sets standards as to how the game should be played. His commandments set a framework around our lives. This framework forms a hedge of protection from evil and from the ill effects of going out of bounds beyond his will for us. When we are tempted to disobey our Coach's instructions we are really questioning whether we can experience greater satisfaction and success by disobeying the Coach than we could by obeying Him. Disobedience sends a message to the Coach that we know more about our role as players than He does as our Coach. As Inventor and Founder of the game of life, He knows exactly what's best for the role of each and every

player. He loves us and is committed to coach us to be the best players and team we can be. He commands our obedience because He knows the devastating effect that sin and disobedience will have on each of us and on the team as a whole: broken lives, failing marriages, bitter disputes, and all sorts of turmoil and anxieties.

3. *He Wants Us to Be Conformed to the Image and Likeness of His Son, Jesus.* This is the Coach's overall purpose for all His players. He wants all of His adopted children to be just like His only begotten Son, who was and is the perfect example of the perfect player in the game of life.

When we passed the entrance exam to the College of Life we received Christ Jesus into our lives and became the Father's adopted child. In position we were already like our heavenly Father's Son, because He was indwelling us in the form of the Holy Spirit. In essence we were instantly transformed into the perfect player—but only in position. It is important to understand the difference between position (or status) and practice. In position we are the perfect example of the perfect player, but in practice we are only a novice, a beginner, or you might say a "lowly freshman" experiencing our first days in the College of Life. Our college career will consist of a lifetime of daily practice. Our goal is eventually to be conformed to the perfect image of the perfect Player. It doesn't happen overnight. It's a lifelong process. In reality we will never reach that state of perfection in our earthly lifetime. The Bible refers to this process as the doctrine of sanctification. Theologically speaking there are three stages of sanctification:

a. *I have been sanctified,* meaning that when I received Christ I immediately was conformed to the image of the Father's Son. That was my "position in Christ."

b. *I am being sanctified,* meaning that in practice I am in the process of being daily conformed to the image of His Son.

c. *I will be sanctified,* meaning that when my College of Life days are over, I will graduate into the very presence of Jesus and be holy and without sin, just as He is. God's number-one purpose for me will then be fulfilled.

The sanctification process will then be complete, and we will indeed be like Jesus in every respect. The truth is we will be perfect and holy, which qualifies us to live eternally with the holy God of the Universe—our heavenly Father. Amazingly enough we will be just as holy as Jesus is holy. From the human view one would say that's impossible, that we can never be as holy as Jesus. But in context that's what the Bible says. That's God's number-one purpose for all who trust in Jesus—for all His children, all of whom are players of the game of life.

Chapter 5

THE NECESSITY OF PREPARATION, TRAINING, AND DISCIPLINE

*All great athletes must get in shape—and stay
in shape—to be winners.*

All great coaches demand the highest degree of discipline from each and every player. The same is true if we are to play the game of life the way the Coach intended for it to be played. We start out as freshmen, eager to learn and develop our skills. We want to live up to our potential and be the best player we can be. We have heard of our Coach's reputation and know He can make and mold us into an integral part of His winning team. After all, He is the God of the Universe and the very Founder of the game of life. He knows what's best to help us develop into the player He wants us to be.

Establishing the Proper Relationship with the Coach

From the very beginning—from the day we responded to the Coach's call to attend the College of Life—we have known we wanted to play for the greatest of all coaches. We have heard of His reputation for being a winner, but we really don't know Him the way He wants us to know Him. He wants us to be the best player of the game of life we can possibly be. The good news is He has a plan for us which He designed before He founded the College of Life, even before the foundation of the world. Just as each member of the

North Carolina Tar Heels basketball team needs to know and establish a close relationship with Roy Williams as his coach, so it is with the players of the game of life. They need to know their Godhead Coach and what he demands of them. The Father, being the first person of the Godhead (Trinity), has provided the players with the perfect example of the perfect player, who is the Father's own Son, Jesus the Christ. He is the second person of the Godhead. Roy Williams has shown his players some exceptional examples of former Tar Heels who made it to the top and are considered to be some of the better players ever to play the game of basketball. Lennie Rosenbluth, Phil Ford, James Worthy, and current three-time all-American Tyler Hansbrough (2008) are just four in this elite group. Probably the greatest of them all was Michael Jordan. Although Jordan was considered the best and most complete of all the players, we must remember he was not perfect. As good an example as he was for us to try to emulate, he had his faults. He was human and had his human frailties. Jesus, on the other hand, was without fault or blemish. He was perfect in every way. He was not only human, but He was also divine at the same time. There has never been and never will be anyone like Him in the future. The Father wants all of His players to pattern their lives after His Son, Jesus. In essence He wants us to surrender our lives to Jesus, so as to allow Him to play the game through us as designed by the Father. Some additional good news: He has provided a Helper to assist us in accomplishing our goal and His purpose. He is the Holy Spirit, or third person of the Godhead. He is closer than our very breath, for He is indwelling each and every player. What a blessing that is! He is known as the Comforter or Helper, whose sovereign purpose is to enable every player on the Coach's team of life to be more like Jesus, the Perfect Player. The player's job is to be willing to be led and trained and molded by the Father Coach. The Holy Spirit's job is to enable us to be the player the Father designed us to be.

So What Is the Coach's Training Process?

In analyzing our Coach's overall game plan we have listed His first three major expectations of us as players of the game of life:

1. To have an intimate relationship with Him.
2. To obey Him as our Coach and leave all the consequences to Him.
3. To be conformed to the likeness and image of His Son, Jesus.

And now we come to His fourth major expectation of us:

4. He wants us to respond to His leading by worshiping and praising Him, and by thanking Him and serving Him.

He wants us to worship and praise Him for who He is, to thank Him for what He has done for us, and to serve Him so as to fulfill His purpose for us as His workmanship. The Bible says, "For we are His workmanship, created in Christ Jesus for good works, which God prepared beforehand that we should walk in them" (Ephesians 2:10).

One of the great lessons I've learned in my journey through this life is that we, as God's children, are called by Him to live a life of response to His overall goodness to us. If we can ever come to the point in our lives when we can fully understand the true nature of our sovereign God and what He has done for us, we will be driven to a natural response of worship, praise, thanksgiving, and service. The more spiritually mature we are in Christ, the more natural and unrestrained we become in responding to His overall goodness. The Bible says that God is love, and that He extends His grace, mercy, and forgiveness to all His children. He is faithful and always keeps His promises. At the same time it is clear that He is also a God of justice. The Bible tells us, "For all have sinned and fall short of the glory of God." (Romans 6:23). It also tells us that, "The wages of sin is death, but the gift of God is eternal life in Christ Jesus our Lord" (Romans 3:23). God demands that our sins be reckoned with. Justice demands that our sin debt be paid in full either by the sinner himself or by the Savior God sent over two thousand years ago to take our place and act as our substitute. To save us from having to pay the death penalty ourselves He paid it for us, for all those who will repent and accept His free gift of salvation. What a gift! What a Savior! By giving you eternal life He "called you out of darkness into His marvelous light" (1 Peter 2:9). He transferred us from death to life—and that's worth more than every treasure on earth. Ephesians 5:8 says: "For you were once darkness, but now you are light in the Lord. Walk as children of light." It's no wonder that we will be motivated to "walk as children of light" and to worship Him, and praise Him, and thank Him, and serve Him! That should be our natural response to His marvelous gift.

The Training Table: Physical Food vs. Spiritual Food

As a general rule the coach demands that all his team members eat at what I came to know as the "training table." When I played basketball at Woodberry Forest School I still remember the initial thrill when I sat down for the first time with the team to eat special food at a special table set aside for the team before each game. As a high school junior at Woodberry Forest School in 1947 I remember thinking to myself, *I'm somebody special! I'm in training. I'm eating special food so I'll be ready for the game!* Actually it wasn't all that special—roast beef, a baked potato, and hot tea. We were drinking hot tea while everyone else was drinking iced tea. Somehow the hot tea set us apart. We were eating and drinking physical food to prepare us to play a physical game against physical opponents. After eating a certain amount we were "full" and didn't want any more. In the game of life it's just the opposite. We eat spiritual food to prepare us for spiritual battles. Strangely enough, the more we eat the more we want to eat. We never get enough. We're never filled to capacity. What is this spiritual food that causes such a strange phenomenon? It's basically partaking and digesting the Rule Book on a daily basis. It's spending sufficient quality time alone in the Coach's presence to establish that intimate personal relationship with the One who wants to show us how the game of life should be played. It's being in daily communication with Him through prayer and meditation that we are able to discern His will for us. This sets the course for our lives to gain the approval of the Coach, thereby guaranteeing our success as a player of the game of life. The moment we accept His free gift of salvation we are given eternal life. By following His rules, our Godhead team of

Coaches promises we will have an abundant life during our earthly existence, and an everlasting life in His presence when our earthly existence is over.

More of My Personal Testimony

The longer I live, the more convinced I am that this spiritual food acts as the true source of a joyful, fulfilled life. Only after I started taking a weekly Bible study course under Ruth Bock in the spring of 1987 did I begin to see the real value of staying in the Word. I had gone to Sunday school and church all my life, and as a youth had even memorized certain key Psalms such as the Twenty-third Psalm and the One Hundredth Psalm, and certain key versus such as John 3:16 and Romans 8:28. In the eighth grade I memorized the list of all thirty-nine books of the Old Testament. Even at that early age I knew something about the Bible, but I really didn't know its contents with any depth of understanding. When I began seriously studying it so as to know what it says, what it means, and what it means to me, the Bible took on new character as well as new meaning. It became relevant in my life. Then when Margaret began leading a class in our home in the fall of 1987, there was no turning back! We both realized we had a spiritual hunger that has increased with every passing year. In January 2000 I began leading our weekly Bible study class, and have been going strong every since. It's absolutely true that the more you eat and digest of the spiritual food of God's Word, the hungrier you get and the more you want. It's a matter of getting a glimpse of the truth as revealed in and through Jesus Christ which then leads to our seeing the need to seek and know more. The more truth we understand, the more we want to understand. The more we desire to understand God's Word, the closer we are drawn into that intimate relationship which He designed us to have with Him.

Margaret and I have been truly blessed in our marriage in that we both have a strong yearning to know our heavenly Father and His Son Jesus on a more personal basis. We have learned that by putting Him first, the more He blesses us, and the stronger our marriage becomes. We are quick to point out the obvious—that we fall short in so many ways each day. The good news is we feel confident we're at least going in the right direction by seeking to know

Him in an increasingly more personal way. I believe, and God's Word confirms it, that if anyone is sincerely willing to seek and know God, He will in His perfect timing reveal Himself to that person. Jeremiah 29:13 states, "You will seek Me and find Me when you search for Me with all your heart." This is a promise of God. He has richly blessed our feeble yet sincere efforts, and I know He will likewise bless any and everyone else who is willing to dedicate himself to the task of developing a personal, intimate relationship with the Sovereign God of the Universe. If you have any doubts, try it and see. You'll be blessed beyond what you can imagine. Margaret and I have never regretted our deeper "walk with the Lord," and we're sure you won't either!

God Requires More than Merely Reading His Word

Bible study is only the beginning point by which we came to know God more intimately. Margaret and I have been blessed to establish a daily devotional and prayer life together. Our general routine is to spend approximately thirty minutes each weekday morning beginning about 6:40 a.m. on our knees. Our weekends vary with circumstances, and sometimes we miss altogether when our schedule varies. But that's our goal: to spend sufficient quality time on a daily basis in communication with our Lord. When we fail to do that, we really miss it, for we have come to appreciate this time together before the Lord.

We take turns reading a daily devotional. At the time of this writing we are using Sarah Young's *Jesus Calling*, which has been marvelous in every way. It is written "to bring you closer to Christ and move your time with Him from a monologue to a dialogue. Each day is written as if Jesus Himself were speaking to you. Because He is." The question is, do we hear Him calling? From time to time we also use *In Touch* by Charles Stanley and David Jeremiah's *Turning Points*. Most of the time our devotional reading is followed by a brief discussion to enable us to share how it applies to our own lives.

The rest of our devotional time together is spent in praying for specific needs. Our general routine is to start with the church universal and then go through a list of churches and their leaders we know and love: Faith Fellowship Church—Randy, Allen, the choir, the Leadership Team, and general ministry needs; then we move on to Grace Fellowship Church and Jason, and Gordon Street Christian Church—Mark, Joanne, and Gail in Kinston; Bogue Banks Baptist; All Saints Episcopal in Morehead City, as well as others that come to mind. Then we start with our family: each of our three children, Elizabeth, Daniel, and Radford, Chad, and "little Virginia"; then Barbara and all of brother Warren's family of four children (Wes, Betty Blaine, Jimbo, and Ashley and spouses) and twelve grandchildren; then Barbara Ruth and all of brother Ely's family of two children (Ruth-E and Ely III and spouses) and six grandchildren. All during this time of prayer, Margaret and I both feel comfortable to interrupt, discuss, or add to the prayers of the one verbalizing. We just carry on a conversation with the Lord as we're led. We then move on to Margaret's sister, "Aunt Carolyn" and her two children, Margaret Wood and Bob, and then her brother, "Uncle Buddy."

After church and family we have a long list of special friends, including our Bible study group, golfing buddies, and so on. At one time or another we have named them all. Time will not permit us to actually name each person every day; the idea is to focus on specific needs of which we may be aware. We don't have to verbalize the same prayer every day, but by being aware of the specific need, the mere mention of the name brings to mind the whole situation that needs attention.

We then move on to praying for our country, from the president on down—the Senate and Congress, the Supreme Court, the war on terrorism, and the brave souls who serve and sacrifice their lives that we might live in freedom. We pray that all our leaders will follow godly principles as they govern us. We pray for our local government and economy and offer a prayer of thanksgiving for how the Lord has raised up Christian men and women to be in positions of leadership throughout our city and county. We believe that the recent good news that is evident in Kinston and Lenoir County is a direct answer to the prayers of the great multitude of prayer warriors who are praying daily for our community, the TransPark, and various ministries that have recently evolved—such as Son Set Ministries, the Refuge, and the Gate. I am convinced that when godly people truly band together in sincere, repentant prayer, God is pleased and will answer according to His highest will for our good.

The next phase of our morning prayer time is directed to praying for specific needs of certain people who are sick, who have lost a loved one, or who are going through dark and challenging times in their lives.

Our last prayers are for each other. I pray for Margaret and she prays for me—for specific needs, our physical health, and our spiritual growth. Margaret and I are continually thankful that the Lord has given us these special times together each morning when we can share devotionals and prayers. Oh, how we have been blessed and are continuing to be blessed! It comes only through God's grace and mercy. We certainly don't deserve it, for each day in so many ways we fall short of who we should be.

Just prior to our devotional and prayer time, I am generally in my home office/study by about 5:30 a.m. or so for approximately an hour and ten minutes of personal quiet time with the Lord. During this special time, there are no distractions—no telephone, no radio, no television, no talking, no nothing—just perfect peace and quiet. It's just "me and the Lord." During this time frame I am drawn by the Holy Spirit into that deeper and more intimate relationship with my heavenly Father that I so desperately need and seek. This special quiet time is set aside for three main purposes:

1. *To write in my private prayer journal.* This generally takes between twelve and fifteen minutes, depending on how fast my thoughts come. When I have something specific in mind before I begin, the words just flow like water. Other times when I'm more contemplative, it takes a few minutes longer. Generally my writing is in the form of a prayer or psalm in which I'm expressing my personal thoughts of praise and thanksgiving as well as particular prayer needs. I always start with the salutation, "Dear Lord." Many times I then follow with something like, "Thank You for getting me up at this early morning hour to allow me to have this time alone with You. I give You all the praise and glory for who You are and how You have blessed Margaret and me and our entire family over the years. Lord, You

are so good to us, and I am so undeserving; yet through Your grace and mercy, You chose to bless us beyond measure. There are many things I don't understand about Your sovereignty and will for my life. Strengthen my faith and trust to truly believe that, according to Romans 8:28, You are engineering my circumstances and causing all things to work together for my good, even those things I don't understand at the present time...." I restrict my journaling to one page per day in a college-ruled composition book, and always end with the words, "In Jesus name. Amen." I am now in my tenth consecutive year of journaling, and I find it to be both refreshing and rewarding in every sense of the word.

2. *To read and study the Bible.* My goal is to read the Bible through during the course of a year on a day-by-day basis. I began doing this on January 1, 1999, at the same time I began journaling. Each year for Christmas Margaret gives me a different version or translation. During the time of this writing in 2008 I am reading Charles Stanley's *Life Application Bible.* This reading generally takes between ten and twenty minutes, but at times it may take as much as forty-five minutes, depending on how much study material is provided for each daily reading. The more I read and study God's Word, the more I learn about God the Father, God the Son, and God the Holy Spirit—and how I relate to each person of the Trinity. The more I learn and know the Bible, the more I am aware of how much I don't know and need to learn.

3. *To study and prepare Bible study lessons.* This time period is usually limited to fifteen to twenty-five minutes, depending on time available. During the summer months when we're not involved in leading a Bible study, I use this time for various other projects or endeavors.

The above time frames are obviously all approximations, for I try not to be legalistic about keeping a rigid structure. I have learned it's best to go with the flow and seek the Lord's leading each day, keeping in mind that circumstances and schedules vary from day to day. I trust the reader will see and understand my true intent in sharing these personal routines. It's certainly not to brag or boast about any spirituality I might have, or to lift me up in any way, because it's not about me. As Randy Spaugh says, "It's all about Jesus." My only purpose is to point out the blessings that come from having consistent daily, quality quiet time with the Lord. This is what I have been led to do, and it certainly has been a blessing to Margaret and me over the years. She also has her own personal routine of reading, studying, and journaling—somewhat different from mine, yet just as rewarding. We give all the praise and glory to God as He leads us. We don't always live up to our own expectations, much less His. We're just thankful for His grace and mercy as He seeks to lead us and we seek to be led by Him on a daily basis.

Chapter 6

THE ADVERSARY COACH

We need to know our opponents' coach, his game plan,
and his track record.

Let's look at North Carolina basketball as compared to the game of life. During the 2007–8 season, UNC played a total of thirty-nine games. Roy Williams coached all thirty-nine of Carolina's games, while each opponent had a different head coach. Strange as it may seem, the same coach coaches each and every opponent we face in the game of life. Just as Roy Williams and his team of coaches receive scouting reports on each opposing team and its coach, our Godhead Coach in the game of life gives us scouting reports on the one coach who coaches each of our opponents. God wants us to know this experienced and seasoned coach, his game plan, strategy, and the tactics he uses for his overall purpose to defeat us in every individual game we play.

The Adversary Coach and Spiritual Warfare

The Rule Book tells us all about our adversary coach. God wants us not only to know his name, but He wants us to know the tools of his trade and how he operates. His name is Satan, otherwise known as the devil. The Bible also refers to him as "the serpent," "Beelzebub," "the ruler of this world," "the prince of the power of the air," and "the evil one." Satan is our enemy. Surveys have revealed that many Christians do not believe in a literal devil. Instead they believe he is a biblical symbol for evil, but that's not the position of the Bible. In our Bible study on Ephesians we learned that the devil is every bit as literal as God is. As the lesson pointed out, it's hard for a symbol to do the things that Scripture attributes to Satan. The Bible makes it clear that the devil is deceiving, murdering, temping, destroying, lying, accusing, and controlling.

First Peter 5:8 cautions us: "Be sober, be vigilant; because your adversary the devil walks about like a roaring lion, seeking whom he may devour." The game of basketball involves a physical battle between two teams, but the game of life is a spiritual war between each individual and Satan and his satanic powers. Ephesians 6:12 describes it this way: "For our struggle is not against flesh and blood, but against the rulers, against the powers, against the world forces of this darkness, against the spiritual forces of wickedness in the heavenly places."

The war against Satan is not only spiritual; it is also strategic. He uses certain devices and well-thought-out methods designed to discourage and defeat us at every turn. If you are a believer in Jesus Christ, you are a target of Satan. His number-one overall purpose is to defeat and even destroy the believer. John 10:10 states, "The thief does not come except to steal and to kill, and to destroy." Jesus, on the other hand, said, "I have come that they may have life, and that they may have it more abundantly." Quite a contrast in objectives!

David Jeremiah says Satan has three goals in attacking Christians:

1. **Destroy the testimony of Christians.** His target is not those who aren't Christians, but those who are.
2. **Destroy the unity of Christian families and homes.** Destroying marriages and homes in this generation is his strategy for weakening the next generation.
3. **Destroy the ministry of Christian churches.** Christians are fighting each other as if their Christian brothers were the enemy. When Christians are divisive and fight against one another, it is because Satan has tricked them into thinking there is another enemy besides him.

John Eldridge makes this important statement about spiritual warfare:

> To live in ignorance of spiritual warfare is the most naïve and dangerous thing a person can do. It's like skipping through the worst part of town, late at night waving your billfold above your head. It's like walking into an Al Qaeda training camp wearing an "I love the United States" T-shirt. It's like swimming with great white sharks, dressed as a wounded sea lion and smeared with blood. And let me tell you something: you don't escape spiritual warfare simply because you choose not to believe it exists or because you refuse to fight it.

David Jeremiah wrote with conviction when he said, "On the authority of Scripture I can tell you that if you are a Spirit-controlled believer in Christ, you are going to experience warfare-related struggles in your life."

PART TWO

Playing the Game of Life

Chapter 7

PLAY BALL! LET THE GAME BEGIN!

*Now that we know the rules, and our Coach has prepared us
for the competition, we're ready to play!*

Let's go back and catch up to the truth. We spent Part One laying the groundwork as if we were preparing to play the game of life for the first time. The truth is that we started playing the game the moment we accepted Christ and made Him the Lord of our lives. At that point we were given eternal life and began playing the game of life. Up until that time we had been playing the game of death.

I well remember my first day in the first grade. I was mainly there to find out what going to school was all about—to begin a period of orientation to get acclimated to this new way of life. It was exciting, but I knew very little about it. I was there at the starting gate, ready to learn to read and write and do arithmetic, and so on. The same is true of the first day I began the College of Life. Although I was going to school, I was merely a baby Christian and was just beginning my lifelong training period of learning to live the life my heavenly Father designed for me. To put it another way, I actually began playing the game of life when I accepted Christ as a twelve-year-old, but I really didn't know much about living the Christian life. Only after a long period of training and disciplined study did my Coach begin to reveal the rules for playing the game. That gradual process (introduced earlier as the "doctrine of sanctification") is required before we can adequately prepare ourselves to meet the everyday challenges, heartaches, and dark times we all face as believers playing the game of life. In this context we move on to the nuts and bolts of playing not only the overall game of life, but also each and every game that comes our way in life's trenches.

A Hard Look at Our Opposition

In our Bible study entitled *Facing the Giants in Your Life*, David Jeremiah lists twelve giants we face on a daily basis, which he calls the "dirty dozen": fear, discouragement, loneliness, worry, guilt, temptation, anger, resentment, doubt, procrastination, failure, and jealousy. Charles Stanley refers to these and similar giants as land mines in the path of the believer. Whether we call them giants or land mines, they are invisible agents of our archenemy, sent to silently entrap the believer as he or she goes about playing the game of life. We need only to look within our churches and our close circle of friends as well as our own lives to see those giants manifesting themselves in one form or another. From time to time most of these giants pop up in the lives of believers. We need to know how to recognize and deal with these adversaries so we can achieve victory as we play the game of life.

We Can Win Every Time

The good news is that we can indeed win every time, if we put these giants and land mines in perspective of who we are in Christ. The Bible tells us plainly, "Greater is He who is in you than he who is in the world" (John 4:4). We need to know for sure and have every confidence that we have the best team and can win every game we play in the game of life. The basis of our confidence is in knowing that the Christ who indwells every believer is greater and more powerful than anything our opponent, Satan, can throw at us. The key is to learn how to appropriate the spiritual power within us. So many Christians never come to realize who they are in Christ. It's like the man who bought the farm in Texas and then through bad management lost it through foreclosure. He never realized he was living on top of one of the world's largest oil reserves. He was poor, yet he was a multibillionaire at the same time…if he had only realized his wealth. Oh, if we as Christians could only realize how rich we are!

When we come to discover our spiritual wealth in having the very Spirit of God living within us, we cannot lose. Our greatest need as players of the game of life is to realize our full potential in Christ. We need to appropriate the fact that "greater is He who is in you than he who is in the world." Always remember, the evil one is continually planting land mines in our path to prevent us from being the children of God our heavenly Father wants us to be.

Let's take a look at the giants we face as we do battle daily with the opposition. We need to know our adversaries before we can properly compete and be victorious. Most of the thoughts and ideas expressed here were gleaned from my notes and the study guide of our David Jeremiah Bible study course, *Facing the Giants in Your Life*, as well as from Charles Stanley's sermons on "Landmines in the Life of a Believer."

The Giant of Fear

Fear has been defined as "a small trickle of doubt that runs through your mind and eventually wears a great channel that all of your thoughts drain into it." God's people are not exempt from living with fear. In fact, reality without fear is impossible. Some lingering fear will always pop up from time to time in any Christian's life. We are fearful for the general well-being of our children; we are fearful for health issues, financial issues, and old-age issues— for example, *What about the future? Will I end up in a nursing home?* Fear can have a devastating effect on anyone who gives in to it.

I am convinced of this one thing: *God does not want us to live in fear.* He wants us to live above it. President Franklin Roosevelt coined the phrase, "The only thing we have to fear is fear itself." The question then becomes, how do we overcome and defeat this giant of fear? When we find ourselves becoming fearful of the future, how does God want us to respond to make it as short lived as possible?

For the Christian, fear demands a biblical response, which I believe entails
a threefold process.

1. ***The key factor is recognizing that the basic cause of any fearful situation
   stems from not believing and trusting in the sovereignty of God.*** In my
   own personal life I am learning more and more (slowly but surely), that
   God is in control, He's in charge, He's sovereign in all circumstances. I'm a
   firm believer in Romans 8:28: "For we know that God causes all things to
   work together for good, to those who love God, for those who are called
   according to His purpose." It is an amazing revelation to realize that God
   is actually engineering everything that seems bad and fearful in my life to
   work together for my good. What a reassuring and comforting thought! If
   my heavenly Father is truly in charge (as I believe He is), and if He wants
   the best for me (as I believe He does), then I need not fear for anything. I
   am set free from the devastating clutches of the giant of fear. "And you shall
   know the truth and the truth shall make you free" (John 8:32).

2. ***Meditate on God's Word and claim God's promises of protection.*** In
   addition to Romans 8:28, etch the following verses in your heart. When
   the spirit of fear begins to move into your life, pull out these verses and
   start to read them. Instead of allowing your mind to be filled with fearful
   lies, fill it with the Word of God.

> Deuteronomy 31:6: "Be strong and of good courage, do not fear
> nor be afraid of them; for the Lord your God, He is the one
> who goes with you. He will not leave you nor forsake you."
>
> Psalm 27:1: The Lord is my light and my salvation; whom shall
> I fear? The Lord is the strength of my life; of whom shall I be
> afraid?
>
> Psalm 118:6: The Lord is on my side; I will not fear. What can
> man do to me?

Proverbs 3:25–26: Do not be afraid of sudden terror, nor of trouble from the wicked when it comes; for the Lord will be your confidence, and will keep your foot from being caught.

Isaiah 41:10: Fear not, for I am with you; be not dismayed, for I am your God. I will strengthen you, yes, I will help you. I will uphold you with My righteous right hand.

2 Timothy 1:7: For God has not given us a spirit of fear, but of power and of love and of a sound mind.

1 John 4:18: There is no fear in love; but perfect love casts out fear, because fear involves torment. But he who fears has not been made perfect in love.

3. ***It takes discipline and right priorities to win the final victory.*** In order to study and meditate on God's Word and fully understand and appropriate the sovereignty of God to the various negative circumstances of our lives, we need to exercise discipline and get our priorities right. We need to have as our number-one goal in life to work toward developing a sense of spiritual maturity. How do we become more spiritually mature? The secret lies in our ability to disadvantage ourselves, purposefully inconvenience ourselves, make ourselves uncomfortable, and even suffer for the goal of achieving a higher purpose. If you think about it, great athletes make these sacrifices in order to become champions in their fields, whether it is football, basketball, golf, or any other sport. They force themselves to practice and condition themselves beyond their comfortable limits to prepare to win the Super Bowl, World Series, U.S. Open, or gold medal. The same is true in your quest to understand the truths of the Bible and become more spiritually mature. The serious Bible student will wake up early or stay up late to read and study the Scripture so as to discover the truth of God's Word.

The question for all of us as we face the giant of fear or any of the other giants we will study is simply this: *how much am I willing to give up or to sacrifice or to make my self uncomfortable to achieve my goal of becoming more spiritually mature?* Remember, the more spiritually mature we are, the better we are able to face and defeat the various giants we will encounter in the game of life.

⌒ The Giant of Discouragement ⌒

To be discouraged means not to approach life with courage; to lose sight of the victory that is ours. No matter who we are or our station in life, we all get discouraged from time to time. The answer to our discouragement is a matter of recognition and response. What makes us vulnerable to discouragement, and how should we respond to it?

Let's look at several factors that make us vulnerable to discouragement:

Fatigue. Someone has said that fatigue makes cowards of us all. No doubt that when we push ourselves too hard, at work or play, to the point of losing sleep, we become worn out and less productive. Then we need to rest and recuperate. In all sports the coach calls time-out not only for a pep talk, but also to give players a time to rest, to be refreshed and recharged before resuming the game. The same is true in the game of life. We become recharged by a pep talk from our Coach, by communing with Him and meditating on His Word.

Frustration. We've been told there are three ways to live life: live out, wear out, or burn out. Our goal should be to live out, certainly not to burn out. People burn out because they work hard without focus, purpose, or accomplishment. It comes from trying to accomplish something that is unattainable, or at least it appears that way from where we stand. We live out our lives when we have a sense of purpose and see our goals being fulfilled. Burnout leads to frustration, an early warning sign of discouragement. Remember that, Jesus, the Light of the world, burns forever. His light never goes out.

Failure. It's easy to see how fatigue and frustration can lead to a feeling of failure. All of us fail from time to time. The key here is to remember that failing is not the issue. It's how we respond to our failure. One of the great lessons I've learned in playing the game of life is that when failure comes, that's the very time we need to praise the Lord anyway. The apostle Paul emphasized this type of positive attitude in his own life when he was able to write, even while in prison, "For I have learned in whatever state I am, to be content" (Philippians 4:11). His attitude of contentment in all things was established many years earlier, as evidenced in his first letter to the church in Thessalonica, when he wrote, "Rejoice always, pray without ceasing, in everything give thanks; for this is the will of God in Christ Jesus for you" (1 Thessalonians 5:16–18). What a blessing it would be if we too could maintain such an attitude when failure comes our way. How we respond to exhaustion and frustration as well as failure makes a big difference regarding our tendency to be discouraged.

Fear. In addition to being a giant in its own right, fear is the final stepping-stone that leads us into the very presence of another giant, the giant of discouragement. When we fail to respond, as Paul advised, to fatigue, frustration, and failure, we become fearful of the future. We don't see any way out. We begin seeing only a bleak picture of what we think will happen. Such a fearful attitude paves the way for the giant of discouragement to defeat us and rob us of the victory that is rightfully ours in Christ.

The Giant of Loneliness

At first glance the giant of loneliness may not seem to be a very formidable foe. We might tend to dismiss its importance with such comments as, "Oh, everybody gets lonely occasionally. I'll get over it. Life will move on." But the truth is, according to some psychiatrists, loneliness has reached epidemic proportions in our modern world. Some say that people today are lonelier than they ever have been in history. It follows that they try to overcompensate for that empty feeling on the inside by filling themselves with alcohol, drugs, food, sex, work, and material things.

The Bible is filled with examples of kings, prophets, and apostles who experience loneliness. In Psalm 102 King David painfully describes his personal loneliness as he was hounded and pursued by a jealous King Saul. He eventually survived it by trusting God in the midst of it. Jeremiah was known as the weeping prophet, because no one would listen to his calls for repentance to avoid the coming destruction of Jerusalem. He was a lonely voice crying in a spiritual wilderness. Even the great apostle Paul was lonely on occasion. In 2 Timothy 4:9–16 he describes how "no one stood with me, but all forsook me." But with his attitude of forgiveness and being content with all things, he was able to state, "May it not be charged against them."

God has provided ways for us to escape our loneliness before it becomes a downward spiral that pulls us down with it. David Jeremiah gives us four ways to defend ourselves from the power of loneliness:

1. *Acknowledge the reality of your loneliness.* There is no shame in a Christian admitting that she or he is lonely. Healing can take place when we admit our loneliness. To deny the reality of the situation only casts us further into the depths of despair.

2. *Accept God's provisions for your loneliness.* The fundamental emptiness in all of us can only be filled by the presence of God Himself. Solving the basic issue of separation from God is the key to any loneliness problem. The first step toward overcoming the negative effects of loneliness is to accept Jesus Christ and be empowered by His Spirit. If we could fully know who we are in Christ, we have the ammunition to defeat the giant of loneliness.

3. *Allow God's Word to fill your heart and mind.* For God's Word to become real in our hearts and be understood by our minds, we must have the Holy Spirit indwelling us. Paul wrote, "But the natural man does not receive the things of the Spirit of God, for they are foolishness to him; nor can he know them because they are spiritually discerned" (1 Corinthians 2:14). It always takes God's influence to help us understand and accept the truth of His Word. Without spiritual discernment, the things of the Spirit of God are "foolishness" to the "natural man." The Gospel of Luke confirms this in writing of Jesus, "And He opened their understanding that they might comprehend the Scriptures" (Luke 24:45).

4. *Activate your network of Christian friends.* Although adverse circumstances might lead us into loneliness, the truth is that we don't have to

linger in the pit. We can choose not to be lonely. The nature of the body of Christ is a source of strength and encouragement. In the average church there are (or should be) many openings or doors through which we can enter into relationships of service and friendship. But we have a choice. We must choose to walk through the door. David Jeremiah gets to the heart of the matter when he writes, "When we have Jesus Christ living in us, though the world may crumble around us, He is the light from on high that thrills and encourages our hearts. Look beyond your circumstances into the face of the One who loves you."

⌒ The Giant of Worry ⌒

Worry is a fruitless experience, a complete waste of time, and yet we all do it. When Jesus tells us, "Therefore do not worry about tomorrow" (Matthew 6:34), He's not saying not to plan for tomorrow, for the Scriptures support the idea of being responsible in our approach to the future. Nor is Jesus saying never to be concerned. What He is saying is that we are not to get worked up over that which we have no control. Worry and anxiety change nothing except the worrier, and always in negative ways. Jesus points out the ineffectiveness of worry when He poses the question, "Which of you by worrying can add one cubit to his stature?" (Matthew 6:27).

But how do we defeat the giant of worry? First, Jesus tells us to focus on only one thing in life: "Seek ye first the kingdom of God and His righteousness." If we do, He promises, "All these things shall be added to you" (Matthew 6:33). Many Christians worry because they know they have violated the priority of seeking God first.

Okay, so we know we shouldn't worry. We know it doesn't do any good, but we do it anyway. The question becomes, how do we keep from worrying? How do we go about defeating this formidable giant of worry?

First, to win over worry, *we need a system of priorities.* A person without priorities will constantly find his or her heart captured by (and worried about) everything that might be. Jesus said to focus on only one thing in life: the kingdom of God and the values for which it stands. If we focus our attention on God and His righteousness, He will supply all our needs. The apostle Paul made it clear: "And my God shall supply all your needs according to His riches in Christ Jesus" (Philippians 4:19).

Second, *we need a strategic program*. The key truth here is to focus only on today. Matthew 6 quotes Jesus as saying, "Therefore do not worry about tomorrow, for tomorrow will worry about its own things. Sufficient for the day is its own trouble." Dale Carnegie advises us to "live in day tight compartments."

So this is our strategy:

1. ***Do not dwell on your tomorrow***. God promises to take care of today, and we can trust Him for that. God said in Deuteronomy 33:25: "As your days, so shall your strength be." That is, God will give you strength as the events of your days require.

2. ***Do not dwell on your yesterdays***. If you have trouble putting certain bad memories of the past out of your mind, remember that God has put our sins as far from us "as the east is from the west" (Psalm 103:12). God has sealed us off from the sins of our past. He made it so that the guilt and shame of them cannot leak into the compartment of today.

David Jeremiah says that when it comes to worrying about yesterdays, he has discovered that people worry about three things: yesterday's sins, yesterday's success, and yesterday's sorrows:

Yesterday's sins. When coming to Christ some people find it difficult to put out of their minds the memories of their past sins. Even though they are forgiven, those memories keep popping back up. They say they know God has forgiven them, but the problem is they can't forgive themselves. All Christians need to trust God and be assured that God has sealed us off from the sins of our past.

Yesterday's successes. One might think that sealing off past successes would be no problem at all, but the truth is that many find it actually harder than sealing off past sins. When we work hard and struggle to reach the top of the ladder of success, the tendency is to keep our focus on our own efforts independent of God. Quite frequently it's hard to switch priorities. The apostle Paul is a good example of one who was on the fast track to success when he met Christ on the road to Damascus. Through the power of the Holy Spirit, he was able to close the door on his past success as a persecutor of Christians to become one of the greatest of all servants of Christ. We too can learn to switch our priorities as Paul did, by "forgetting those things which are behind" (Philippians 3:13).

Yesterday's sorrows. Many times we find it difficult to seal off the sorrow that lingers after tragedies and heartaches, which may be even harder than putting our sins and successes behind us. Whenever yesterday's sorrows linger too long in our mind and heart, the best way to overcome it is to learn to live in the presence of Almighty God and identify with Him who suffered the greatest sorrow imaginable. He willingly gave His only Son, who was sinless in every way, as a sacrifice for the sins of the world. Jesus paid a debt He did not owe for all of us who owed a debt we could not pay. What an unimaginable sorrow He must have experienced, and yet He did it for all of us—for you and for me. If we could only let the true reality of that fact pierce our conscious awareness, we would be compelled to respond with thanksgiving and praise to our heavenly Father.

> **Insight:** Practicing the presence of God in our lives on a daily basis is the key to overcoming our worries about yesterday, today, and tomorrow.

⌒ The Giant of Guilt ⌒

A guilty conscience left unresolved can be devastating to the unbeliever as well as the believer. Two things are necessary for defeating the giant of guilt: learning or recognizing the cause of our guilt, and learning how to remove it. One of the best biblical examples of dealing with guilt is that of King David and his adultery with Bathsheba. In his attempt to cover up his sin of adultery, David committed an additional sin of arranging the murder of Bathsheba's husband, Uriah. While concealing his sins David later described his agony of guilt and anguish of body and soul when he wrote, "When I kept silent, my bones grew old through my groaning all the day long" (Psalm 32:3). The Lord revealed to the prophet Nathan what he needed to know so as to confront David with his sins. David's admission and plea for mercy is an example for us all: "Have mercy on me. O God, according to your loving kindness; according to the multitude of your tender mercies, blot out my transgressions. Wash me thoroughly from my iniquity, and cleanse me from my sin. For I acknowledge my transgressions, and my sin is ever before me" (Psalm 51:1–3).

David gave us the pattern for defeating the giant of guilt in our own lives: he accepted full responsibility for his sin, he acknowledged the sinfulness of sin, and he addressed his confession to God. If the confession of sin is the bad news, then the removal of sin is the good news. Because of his close relationship with his Father God prior to his sin, David was able to come boldly and ask Him to "blot out all my iniquities." He sincerely desired to be washed and cleansed and purged of all his sins.

After his sins were blotted out, David sought to have his joy in the Lord restored. He prayed, "Make me hear joy and gladness, that the bones You have broken may rejoice.... Restore to me the joy of Your salvation, and uphold me with Your generous Spirit" (Psalm 51:8, 12). Notice that David was not asking for God to restore his salvation, but rather to restore the joy of his salvation. God had described David as "a man after His own heart" (1 Samuel 13:14). David's sin caused him to lose his fellowship with God, but not his relationship with God. The same is true when a Christian sins; she or he gets out of fellowship with God, but doesn't lose the relationship with God. A believer who truly trusts in Jesus for salvation becomes a child of God forever, and that salvation is forever sealed by the Holy Spirit. Relating to the human level, my earthly father was Ely Jackson Perry Sr. Just because I may have displeased him from time to time did not make me any less his son. Our father-son relationship could never be broken. Any disobedience on my part could take us out of our fellowship with each other (until restored), but not out of our relationship, which can never be destroyed. He will always be my father.

After David's fellowship with God is restored, he begins to focus on the future. In Psalm 51:12 he prays to be upheld by God's Spirit. Never again does he want to fail like he failed with Bathsheba and Uriah.

When you and I sin, we can defeat the giant of guilt by accepting responsibility, acknowledging the sinfulness of our sin, and addressing our confession to God. If we do these three things, our sins will be erased, our joy restored, and our fellowship renewed.

> **Insight:** To put it in perspective, guilt can be a good thing by reminding us we have sinned. It serves as a motivation to help us regain a clear conscience.

⌒ The Giant of Temptation ⌒

The playwright Oscar Wilde wrote, "I can resist everything except temptation." Temptation is a constant foe for all of us, no matter who we are. Fortunately, for all of us playing the game of life, God has provided a way of escape from the giant of temptation.

Temptation in itself is not a sin. All the great characters of the Bible, from Genesis to Revelation, were tempted. Even Jesus Himself was "one who has been tempted in all things as we are, yet without sin" (Hebrews 4:15). We've all heard the excuses: "The devil made me do it," and "It was more than I could handle." Actually, the truth is that all temptation is under God's control, and He does not allow us any more than we can handle and resist with His help. From the human perspective, most people would prefer that life be free of any temptation. But from God's view, if this were true we would never be able to demonstrate our love for the Lord Jesus Christ, and God would receive no glory from our decision to resist temptation and obey Him instead. When we make a decision to resist temptation, God is glorified. In his first letter to the church in Corinth, Paul writes, "God is faithful, who will not allow you to be tempted beyond what you are able [to resist], but with the temptation will provide the way of escape also, that you may be able to endure it" (1 Corinthians 10:13).

David Jeremiah makes a keen observation when he writes, "One of the things I have been learning as I get older is that temptation is not so much a matter of what we don't do as much as a matter of *who we love*. When we come to know Jesus, and we cultivate within our hearts a relationship of intimacy with Him, that in itself will keep us from many faults and sins." The more intimate our relationship is with Jesus, the easier it is to see and follow the way of escape that He provides for us when we are tempted to go astray.

David Jeremiah offers seven practical suggestions to help us choose the way of escape as we seek to defeat the giant of temptation:

1. ***Recognize the possibility of temptation.*** Woe to the person who pridefully believes he is immune from temptation ("Pride goeth before destruction" [Proverbs 16:18]).

2. ***Request help in advance of temptation.*** The best preparation for spiritual conflict is accomplished before the battle begins ("Lead us not into temptation" [Matthew 6:13]).

3. ***Resist the devil, and he will flee from you.*** Submitting to the Word of God as Jesus did in resisting Satan's temptation in the wilderness is the key factor in resisting the devil. Jesus resisted by saying, "Be gone Satan! For as it is written, you shall worship the Lord your God and serve Him only" (Matthew 4:10).

4. ***Retreat from certain kinds of temptation.*** The Bible tells us we should flee from three kinds of temptation: idolatry, immorality, and greed. Joseph is the perfect example when he ran from the immoral advances of Potiphar's wife.

5. ***Remove any means of sin from you.*** Romans 13:14 says to "make no provisions for the flesh, to fulfill its lust." Put yourself in a place where it's not possible to sin.

6. ***Replace bad influences with good ones.*** We are wise to spend time with godly people. On the other hand, how are we to win others for Christ if we don't spend time with non-Christians? It takes a mature Christian to know the answer.

7. ***Resolve to live on the high road.*** The high road is not free of temptation or spiritual pitfalls, but it is the road on which God promised to give you a way of escape. When we choose the way God provides, the giant of temptation will flee.

⮞ The Giant of Anger ⮜

There are two kinds of anger: sinless anger and sinful anger. Ephesians 4:26 says, "Be angry, and so not sin; do not let the sun go down on your wrath." A good example of righteous indignation, or sinless anger, is when Jesus over-turned the tables of the moneychangers in the temple because of their injus-tice toward worshipers. Jesus' anger was always directed toward the injustice and unrighteousness of others, not about Himself. Even when He was being crucified, he expressed forgiveness and not anger toward His murderers. Sinful anger, on the other hand, arouses resentment, bitterness, and unforgiveness.

David Jeremiah points out five ways to avoid being defeated by the giant of anger:

1. ***Don't nurse your anger.*** When we choose not to get rid of anger, the danger is it will turn into something worse. Anger turns into resentment, which leads to bitterness, which leads to unforgiveness, which turns into a defiled conscience.
2. ***Don't rehearse your anger.*** Don't make anger a part of your conversation. Re-verbalizing our anger just makes the roots of that anger deepen into our heart.
3. ***Don't converse about your anger.*** Ephesians 4:29 says, "Let no unwhole-some word proceed from your mouth." The word for unwholesome means "corrupt" or "cutting." Sarcasm when carried too far can be unwholesome in that sense.
4. ***Don't disperse your anger.*** Sinful anger is displayed when we throw a temper tantrum when we don't get what we want. Young children are known to do this quite frequently. Some adults are not above such behavior.
5. ***Do reverse your anger.*** Instead of nursing, rehearsing, conversing about,

and dispersing our anger, we need to reverse our anger before it hurts us and others. Ephesians 4:32 gives us the solution: "Be kind to one another, tenderhearted, forgiving one another, just as God in Christ also forgives you." Paul is saying the way to reverse anger is to do it with forgiveness, loving-kindness, and tenderness. You are to go to the person toward whom you have directed your anger and then minister to that person. Love them in the way that God in Christ has loved us.

When you find yourself angry at someone, slay the giant of anger with the tender action of forgiving love. That's the weapon that the giant of anger cannot withstand.

⌒ The Giant of Resentment ⌒

The tiny seed of resentment, if not uprooted early on, can blossom into a full-blown state of bitterness or rebellion. Resentment may be among the most deceptive of the giants hiding in the forest of our lives. Unlike anger, which is generally more impulsive and sudden, resentment builds slowly and gradually over time. Accumulated resentment can lead in time to anger and bitterness—and even violence. The giant of resentment needs to be banished immediately from our lives when it is first detected.

In our Bible study, we learned five steps to defeating resentment:

1. ***Think it through***. Step back from the trees and try to get a picture of the whole forest. Is holding in our resentment really worth the destruction that follows?
2. ***Write it down***. By writing down on paper the reason you are resentful, it will sound totally different to you than when you rehearse it in your mind.
3. ***Work it out***. Physical exercise can be as good for your soul as it is for your body. Research has shown that people who get regular physical exercise handle conflicts better than those who don't.
4. ***Talk it over***. The Lord Jesus Christ should be our best friend. It's wonderful to be able to talk to Him on a personal basis. Tell Him specifically

about your resentments. It's hard to remain bitter and resentful while sitting in the presence of the Lord.

5. ***Give it up***. God's method for getting rid of resentment is through love and forgiveness. His proven way will work for us, too.

Working through these five steps will guarantee victory over the giant of resentment. You cannot lose. It's worked for many, and it will work for you and for me.

⌒ The Giant of Doubt ⌒

Doubting the truth is not a sin, but the problem is that if not properly handled, such doubt can lead to despair, or worse. Doubt can be both good and bad. On the negative side it can keep us away from discovering the truth. On the positive side it can motivate us to dig deep and discover the truth. All of us have faced the giant of doubt from time to time. It should be comforting to us struggling with this giant to know that many of the great men of the Bible also had doubts. Many of David's psalms cried out with uncertainties to God. The central theme of the book of Ecclesiastes expresses what Solomon considered the uncertainty of the reality of life. Jesus called John the Baptist the "greatest of all the prophets," and yet John had his doubts about the Messiah. Even after John himself baptized Jesus and heard the Father proclaimed that He was His beloved Son, John plainly asked Jesus, "Are You the Coming One, or do we look for another?" (Matthew 11:3).

The greatest doubter in the Bible was Thomas, one of Jesus' disciples, often referred to as "Doubting Thomas." After Jesus was crucified and had risen from the grave, some of the other disciples told Thomas they had "seen the Lord." Expressing his doubts Thomas said to them, "Unless I see in His hands the print of the nails, and put my finger into the print of the nails, and put my hands into His side, I will not believe" (John 20:25). In expressing his doubt Thomas was verbalizing his desire for evidence. God is not afraid of our questions, but He wants us to delve further to pursue the truth. In our quest for answers and evidence, we ultimately must come in contact with a person:

the Lord Jesus Christ. That's what happened to Thomas. His sincere doubts led him to seek truth and answers about Jesus. He wanted to know the truth, and Jesus led him there. "Then He said to Thomas, 'Reach your finger here and look at my hands; and reach your hand here, and put it into My side. Do not be unbelieving, but believe'" (John 20:27). The Scripture does not tell us whether or not Thomas actually felt Jesus' hands and side. The next verse merely says, "And Thomas answered and said to Him, 'My Lord and my God'" (John 20:28). Jesus led him from honest doubt to truthful belief. You see, Christianity is not about doctrines and creeds. It's about Christ and having a relationship with Him. I learned years ago that Christianity is not a religion; it's a relationship.

When fighting the giant of doubt in the game of life, the best place to start is with honesty. We need to admit we have doubts. Verbalize them carefully not only to ourselves but also to a trusted friend. Some may doubt the accuracy of the Bible, the reality of the resurrection, or the existence of heaven or hell. Others find it hard to believe that the only way to God is through Christ.

What's the answer to our honest doubts? Let me suggest two things to keep in mind:

Acknowledge your doubts prayerfully. I believe that the most important thing is to turn our doubts into prayers to God. The good news is that He already knows our doubts. We are not telling Him to inform Him, but He will use our conversation with Him to strengthen our faith and lead us to the truth. If we honestly seek the truth from Him, He will reveal it to us in His perfect timing. I'm thoroughly convinced of that. Just remember: we're on His timetable and not ours.

Accept your limitations humbly. The older I get and the more I learn, the more I discover I don't know. I want to know the truth about God and my relationship with Him through His Son. The key is to pray and keep on praying until He reveals it to us in His time. I believe the Bible has the answers to every important need we have in life. Someone said, "Everything in the Bible is true, but not all truth is in the Bible." The Bible was not given to us as an encyclopedia or textbook to answer every question in the world, but it was given to us so that we might know the most important thing in life: *to know God and to receive eternal life through faith in His Son.*

The bottom line is that during our earthly existence we will never completely understand God and all His ways, because we are not supposed to. As finite human beings we were not designed to know everything about our infinite God. Don't worry about your doubts and what you don't know, but use doubt as a tool to draw you closer to the truth.

⌒ The Giant of Procrastination ⌒

The most dangerous word in the Bible might be the word "tomorrow," an observer once noted. Why? Because that word has the ability to rob dreamers of their dreams. It has kept more people from coming to Christ and finding salvation than any other word in the dictionary. It happens to be Satan's favorite word. If he can delay until tomorrow your thinking about salvation, he's got you right where he wants you. It's the same principle used by the gas station operator who put up the eye-catching sign, "Free gas tomorrow." God's favorite word is "today," as in "Today is the day to be saved" (2 Corinthians 6:2).

In our day-to-day lives we can identify with putting things off until tomorrow—writing a thank-you letter, calling a friend, or visiting the nursing home. It's called "procrastination," and most all of us are guilty of it, some more than others. The act of succeeding has been defined as "knowing what to do and when to do it—and doing it at the moment." Thomas Huxley had it right when he came to understanding procrastination: "The most important result of all education is to make you do the things you have to do, when it ought to be done, whether you like it or not." What is the lesson to be learned? *To do the things you have to do when they have to be done.*

Procrastination is not only dangerous in the realm of salvation and rendering godly service; it can also be harmful in every area of life if allowed to take over and continue. We all have our favorite procrastinations: cleaning up clutter (this is mine personally), dieting, exercising, stopping smoking, stopping drinking too much, doing jobs around the house ... the list goes on.

But salvation is the most important. "Do not boast about tomorrow, for you do not know what a day may bring" (Proverbs 27:1). "Whereas you do not know what will happen tomorrow. For what is your life? It is even a vapor that appears for a little time and then vanishes away" (James 4:14).

You do not know what tomorrow will bring. Tomorrow may never come. Today is the day of salvation.

⇜ The Giant of Failure ⇝

The lesson to be learned as we battle with the giant of failure is that failure can be a stepping-stone to success. Just because you may have failed at something does not mean you're a failure. Life is filled with failures, whether in athletics, politics, or your personal life. Seeing failure from God's perspective helps us to profit from it.

Stephen Pile, in his book *The Incomplete Book of Failures*, lists failures of some people who later became successful:

- *Beethoven,* whose teacher called him hopeless as a composer.
- *Walt Disney,* who went bankrupt several times before he built Disneyland.
- *Thomas Edison,* whose teacher said he was too stupid to learn anything.
- *Albert Einstein,* who did not speak until he was seven. His teacher described him as mentally slow and unsociable. He was expelled and refused admittance to the Zurich Polytechnic School.
- *Henry Ford,* who failed and went broke five times before he finally succeeded.
- *Winston Churchill,* who failed the sixth grade. He had many failures and setbacks before he became prime minister of England at age sixty-two.

Just because you are a Christian does not mean your spiritual growth will be without failures. Jesus' disciples had plenty of failures along the way. Jesus Himself said, "The spirit indeed is willing, but the flesh is weak" (Matthew 26:41). The famous Scottish preacher Alexander Whyte described spiritual growth like this: "Spiritual growth is the saints falling down and getting up, falling down and getting up, falling down and getting up, all the way to heaven." I think we all can identify with that, for we all have had our ups and downs. The good news is that it's all right to fall, just as long as you get up and are headed in the right direction.

God allows His children to fail for a good purpose. We fail now that we might succeed later. We fail in the incidental so that we might succeed in the important. We fail in the temporary so that we might succeed in the eternal. Our failures in time prepare us for success in eternity! We fail outwardly so that we might succeed inwardly. Peter Marshall said, "It is better to fail in a cause that will ultimately fail." The question I am learning to ask is simply this: "Lord, what are You trying to teach me through my failure?"

What is the best way to fight the giant of failure? Here are six suggestions we learned from our Bible study:

1. *Acknowledge your failure.* Most of us hesitate to admit failure because we think of it as confessing sin. All sin is a failure of some sort, but not all failure is sin. Remember, just because you may have failed at something does not mean you are a failure. It took me some fifty years to admit in public that I failed the bar exam the first time I took it. I had always considered it a stigma of failure and weakness. I was afraid to share my failure with others because I felt they might think less of me. Only when we studied the giant of failure did I first openly reveal this fact to anyone. The result was a freedom and release that was both refreshing and maturing.

2. *Accept God's forgiveness.* If our failure is due to sin, the only way to overcome its effect is to confess it to God and receive His forgiveness. "If we confess our sins, He is faithful and just to forgive us our sins and to cleanse us from all unrighteousness" (John 1:9). To continue holding in an unconfessed, unforgiven sin can be devastating in the life of any believer.

3. *Use failure as a step toward success.* We can all learn this lesson from inventor Thomas Edison. When an assistant tried to console him after a string of failed experiments had produced no results, Edison replied, "Oh,

we have lots of results. We know seven hundred things that won't work!" By studying our failures we can discover what we are doing wrong, which can only lead us more quickly to what to do right.

4. ***Accept failure as a fact of life, not a way of life.*** Failure is an event, not a person; failure is something that happens, not someone you become. A good example is Peter's denial of Jesus, not once but three times. Peter failed, but he was not a failure. By renewing his focus on his Lord and Savior, Peter later became remembered as one of Jesus' closest followers, preaching the gospel message with fiery commitment.

5. ***Arise from failure and start again.*** When we fail, Satan wants us to wallow in self-pity, to sulk and to feel sorry for ourselves. The best thing you can do is stand up, brush yourself off, and start moving forward again. From our study of Jonah we learned that God is a God of second chances. Jonah failed miserably when God told him to go to the wicked city of Nineveh to preach repentance. Instead of preaching he ran the opposite way. Jonah 3:1–2 records God's response: "Now the word of the Lord came to Jonah the second time saying, 'Arise, go to Nineveh, that great city, and preach to it, the message that I told you.'"

6. ***Avoid judging others on their failure.*** Some people may give the appearance of being a failure, when in reality God sees their potential and leads them to succeed. We've already mentioned the likes of Beethoven, Disney, Edison, Einstein, Ford, and Churchill. The Bible provides three noteworthy stories that serve to warn us about judging others who seem to be failures.

- The rich man and Lazarus in Luke 16. Outwardly the rich man was the success, and poor Lazarus, because of his poverty, was a failure. Yet in God's eyes exactly the opposite was true. The rich man ended up in agony, and Lazarus ended up comforted in Paradise.

- The Pharisee and the tax collector in Luke 18. Outwardly the Pharisee was the epitome of success, but because of his arrogance and pride, in God's eyes he was judged to be a failure. The tax collector, holding one of the most despised jobs, was judged as being a success because he was humble and repentant.

- Simon the Pharisee and the prostitute in Luke 7. Simon, who was rich, invited Jesus for dinner in his home. Simon was offended by the prostitute's impropriety when she anointed Jesus' feet with perfume and her tears. On the other hand Jesus was offended by Simon's lack of love.

⌒ The Giant of Jealousy ⌒

Jealousy has been called a strange animal. It can be either positive or negative. When we are jealous *for* another, we have their best interest at heart. When we are jealous *of* another, we're embarking on a selfish journey that can only end in travail. The lesson to learn is that jealousy of another is a sin to be avoided.

Shakespeare called jealousy the "green sickness." To be jealous means to strike out at what somebody else is or what somebody else has. On the other hand, Scripture says that we are to "rejoice with those who rejoice, and weep with those who weep" (Romans 12:15). The jealous person does just the opposite. How many of us can dig deep into our hearts and identify with that? How many of us have ever been glad when an acquaintance suffered a setback (because it "serves them right"), or been green with envy at the success of a friend or competitor?

As a general rule, wealth envies wealth and power envies power—a situation that holds true in churches as well as in the political realm. Jealousy travels in performance circles and professional circles as well as in personal circles. Biblical examples include Jacob's and Esau's jealousy of each other. Joseph's brothers jealousy of him, and King Saul's jealousy of David.

We all need to be on guard, because when jealousy comes in the front door, love goes out the back door. Above all else, jealousy always does two things: it destroys others and it destroys us. While acknowledging that jealousy and envy are destructive attitudes, the question is: how can we conquer them?

When we are tempted to be jealous and envious of someone, we must remember that we have a choice as to how we shall respond. Satan tempts us to respond to situations with jealousy and envy, but we don't have to give in. God gives us a choice.

In our strategy for conquering the giant of jealousy, our Bible study suggested four things to do:

1. ***Renounce jealousy as a sin***. The Scriptures are clear that the Pharisees' sin of envy resulted in Jesus' being handed over and put to death. "For He knew that because of envy they delivered Him" (Matthew 27:15). "For He knew that the chief priest had handed Him over because of envy" (Mark 15:10). First and foremost, jealousy must be renounced as a sin.

2. ***Remember your rival in prayer***. When we find ourselves envious or jealous of another person, the best thing we can do is pray for that person and thank God for his success or good fortune or whatever is the source of our envy. Even if it's hard to do and your heart is not in it, pray for them anyway, and ask God to help you to be sincere as you pray. It's amazing how the Lord will answer your prayers by blessing you as well as your rival. This approach has worked in my own life, and I know it will work for you.

3. ***Reaffirm God's goodness to you***. Our jealousy of other people comes from wanting the blessings God has given them. We don't understand why He has blessed them and not us, and we become jealous of what they have that we don't have. We all have been blessed far beyond what we deserve, because not one of us actually deserves anything; only through God's grace and mercy are we even alive. When we begin to count our own blessings, continuing in a jealous frame of mind toward another becomes more difficult. As David Jeremiah says, "Thanksgiving will douse the spark of jealousy and fan the flames of gratitude every time."

4. ***Rekindle God's love in your heart***. How do you rekindle God's love in your heart? By reading His Word and through prayer. Purpose in your heart to practice the principle of positive replacement, by replacing envy with love. Where love is, envy cannot abide. First Corinthians 13:4 holds the key to defeating the giant of jealousy: "Love does not envy."

The Road to Victory

This brings us to the end of our study of the twelve basic opponents we all face in the game of life. We have referred to these adversaries as giants or landmines in the path of the believer.

Here are five thoughts to keep in mind that will help us be victorious as we battle these giants:

1. Make Jesus Christ the spiritual giant of your life, for He will fill you with love, joy, and gratitude as well as direction for victory.
2. When His love fills your heart, it will push out the jealousies and envies of life that hinder your success in battle.
3. Keep in constant communication with your Coach through daily prayer and meditation. Refer to His Rule Book daily. Let His Word abide in you.
4. The bottom-line key to victory is time: time alone with God, your Coach—and not just time, but quality time... *sufficient* quality time.
5. As we battle each of these giants, always remember we're in a spiritual war, not a physical war. In essence, the battle is not ours, but God's. "Thanks be to God, who gives us the victory through our Lord Jesus Christ" (1 Corinthians 15:57).

Chapter 8

LEARNING FROM OUR ADVERSITIES

We've spent considerable time discussing the twelve giants we face as Christians and players of the game of life. We've talked about Satan as being our number-one enemy and how he uses these giants to act as land mines in our path to cause trouble, trials, and adversities—all designed by Satan for the single purpose of causing us suffering and pain. When these dark times come, it's easy to wonder: *Where is God? Is He letting me down? If God is good, why is He letting me go through all this? Why is He allowing evil to triumph?* We might further ask: *is God punishing me?* When we feel that God is not to be found, or that He doesn't care about our dark times, that's when it really hurts and it is difficult to endure.

Trials Have Several Sources

When the going gets rough, it helps to look at our hardships from a biblical perspective. From God's Word we learn that trials come from many sources. Let's look at five.

1. ***Trials can be the natural consequences of our own sin.*** If we break a criminal law we should expect to suffer the legal consequences. If we don't watch our diet and we make gluttons of ourselves, we can expect to reap the results of an unhealthy lifestyle. If we act selfishly in our marriage, we can expect to have a less than satisfying relationship.

2. ***God causes and uses some trials as a program of discipline for us.*** Just as earthly parents train their children with parental discipline to help them discern between right and wrong behavior, so our heavenly Father disciplines His children to help us discern His will for their lives.

3. ***Some trials are direct attacks from Satan.*** Most if not all of the twelve giants we face in the game of life can be caused and used by Satan to defeat us. Job and Paul both experienced numerous satanic attacks. Both were considered exceptionally righteous men. Both emerged victorious, as can you and I.

4. ***Some adversities are caused by natural disaster.*** God can use a hurricane, flood, or fire to cause us to count our blessings and draw us closer to Him.

5. ***Other trials can result from our own foolish, although not necessarily sinful, action.*** We can make foolish decisions while dealing in the stock market. We can make poor choices in the company we keep, or by failing to seek sound advice in preparing for the future. God in His sovereignty has chosen to give us a certain amount of free will in certain situations. Along with that freedom to act on our own, He also gives us a mind with which to think and make decisions.

The Key to Overcoming Adversity

Many writers and orators have noted that the winds of adversity blow strongly in every direction. Eventually we all feel the weight of some severe trial, hardship, misfortune, or setback. The question is, how do we overcome it? How can we be victorious over adversity?

The key to overcoming any adversity boils down to one thing: the proper response. But what is the proper response? The first questions I'm learning to ask myself when adversity strikes are: *Lord, what are you trying to show me? What are you trying to teach me? What do you want me to learn from all this? What are you up to in my life?* I'm convinced that if we look at each adversity or trial from God's perspective, we would discover that all the bad things that come our way have a purpose. God allows them so that we can learn from them. No matter what the cause, a lesson is available for us to learn. Adversity can be, as someone once said, "a setback from which we can take our greatest leap forward."

Have you ever noticed that some people are devastated by trials while others stand in the confidence of God's faithfulness? Their response reveals an overwhelming sense of stability and strength. They just know in their heart that God is going to see them through their heartache and bring them out on the other side a more mature person. In the midst of their trial they are able to give praise and thanksgiving to their sovereign God, with the expectation of learning and growing from the experience. You can see peace and contentment in their very countenance, even in the deepest part of the valley. That is not to say that in any way they overdo or exaggerate their confidence in the Lord to the point of laughing off adversity without due regard for a godly response. In certain situations there needs to be a time of grieving or a time for merely lending a sympathetic ear. Solomon wrote, "To everything there is a season, a time for every purpose under heaven: ... a time to weep and a time to laugh, a time to morn and a time to dance" (Ecclesiastes 3:1–4). The response we're talking about is one of quiet confidence in God's grace, knowing that all is well, even in the midst of one's adversity. Consider Paul's earnest prayer that God would remove a certain adversity he called "a thorn in the flesh":

> Concerning this thing I pleaded with the Lord three times it might depart from me. And He said to me, "My grace is sufficient for you, for My strength is made perfect in weakness." Therefore most gladly I will rather boast in my infirmities that the power of Christ may rest upon me. Therefore I take pleasure in infirmities, in reproaches, in needs, in persecution, in distress, for Christ's sake. For when I am weak, then I am strong. (2 Corinthians 12:8–10)

Are you and I able to accept our adversities, our thorns in the flesh, and rest in the same confidence and assurance as Paul that God's "grace is sufficient for us"? Are we able to "gladly ... boast in [our] infirmities, that the power of Christ may rest upon [us]"? Are we able to "take pleasure in infirmities, in reproach, in needs, in persecution, in distress, for Christ sake"? Paul did it, and with the right attitude, you and I can learn to do the same. Most would say, "Oh, no. That's impossible and not even human! I could never be glad or take pleasure in the fact that I am burdened with the adversity or trial I'm going through." I choose to think that it can be done, but it takes the right attitude and a certain level of maturity in Christ to be able to rest in the assurance that God's grace is sufficient for me. That's my goal. I have a long way to go, but I'm still working on it!

The Importance of Attitude

From one of my mentors, Charles Swindoll, here's a quote that zeros in on the importance of our attitude in responding to the various giants we face:

> The longer I live, the more I realize the impact of attitude on life. Attitude, to me, is more important than facts. It is more important than the past, than education, than money, than circumstances, than failures, than successes, than what other people think or say or do. It is more important than appearances, giftedness, or skill. It will make or break a company ... a church ... a home. The remarkable thing is we have a choice every day regarding the attitude we will embrace for that day. We cannot change our past.... We cannot change the fact that people will act in a certain way. We cannot change the inevitable. The only thing we can do is play on the one string we have, and that is attitude.... I am convinced that life is 10 percent what happens to me and 90 percent how I react to it. And so it is with you.... We are in charge of our attitudes.

If you think about it, Swindoll made a great point about the importance of having the right attitude. That's one thing I've been working on, or trying to work on. I've known for a long time that none of the twelve giants from the last chapter can actually hurt you. Go back and review each one, beginning with fear and discouragement... on through to failure and jealousy. Fear itself can't hurt you; it's how we react or respond to our circumstances that causes the problem. Discouragement in itself can't hurt you; it's our poor response and reaction to the gloomy circumstances that cause the stress, tension, and worry that lead to discouragement. With the proper attitude we can literally choose to overcome any and all of these giants.

We Can Learn from Young David

David provided one of the greatest examples of the right attitude and proper response when confronted with seemingly impossible odds. He was a young shepherd boy facing a literal giant. Goliath was the champion of the Philistines, the archenemy of Israel and King Saul. Goliath had challenged the Israelites to choose their best man to meet him in battle, one on one. The nation of the loser would serve the nation of the winner. No Israelite would step forward to meet the challenger. It looked like all was lost until David volunteered to battle the giant. He was too young to be in the king's army. He just happened to be on hand after bringing food and supplies from his father to his brothers serving on the frontline.

Why did little David step forward? Why did he think he could conquer such a formidable foe? What was on his mind? The answer is found in his attitude, background, and close relationship with his God. The account is recorded in 1 Samuel 17, where we see God's supernatural strength in action in the life of David. Let's look at his attitude as he faced Goliath.

David never considered defeat as an option. He recalled his past victories and God's faithfulness. David recalled how God had strengthened him in the past to kill a lion and a bear, and he expected the same sort of help to strengthen him against Goliath. Most of all, David realized he could not win on his own strength. He knew God had to be with him and act through him or he would suffer defeat. In reading the account, note that David's brothers mocked him. King Saul pacified him. Goliath made fun of him. But their negative talk did not affect David. He choose five smooth stones and a slingshot as his weapons instead of the body armor of Saul. For David, the size of the giant was irrelevant. He faced Goliath clothed in the strong faith of the living God. David's attitude was one of trust and complete confidence in the God who had proven Himself to be faithful in the past.

Read what the Scripture says as little David stood before the giant Goliath and warned him that the Philistines were defying the God of Israel:

> Then David said to the Philistines, "You come to me with a sword, with a spear, and with a javelin. But I come to you in the name of the Lord of hosts, the God of the armies of Israel, whom you have defied. This day the Lord will deliver you into my hand, and I will strike you and take your head from you.... Then all this assembly shall know that the Lord does not save with sword and spear; for the battle is the Lord's, and He will give you into our hands." (1 Samuel 17:45–47)

What an attitude of confidence—not in his own ability, but in God's sovereign power! God had prepared him in advance for the challenge. David was submissive to His will, knowing in his heart that he would prevail and slay the giant. You and I can develop that same attitude of confidence and trust in God's grace and mercy and sovereign power. The question is, how? How do we go about developing such an attitude to enable us to defeat the giants in our lives?

The answer is it takes time—sufficient quality time of being in His presence, reading and studying His Word, and seeking His will through prayer and communion with the sovereign God of the Universe. As a shepherd boy David spent many hours alone with God. During these times of communication and interaction, God's plan and purpose for his life was revealed to him. When not actively tending his sheep he spent much of his time in quiet meditation on the hillsides playing his harp and listening to the Lord speak to him. This is the kind of quiet time you and I need to achieve the attitude of confidence and assurance that God is in control and that He will see us through every adversity as we face each of the twelve giants that come our way. Remember, none of these giants can defeat us if we have the right attitude. Can we say with David, "I come to you in the name of the Lord, and I will prevail against you, for the battle is the Lord's and He will give you into our hands?"

The Advantages of Adversities

At first glance a lot of people tend to associate the word "adversity" with something bad or negative. They think of adversity as a stumbling block and something that stands in the way of success and happiness. But for others who approach adversity with the right attitude, it can be a source of spiritual growth and maturity. Adversity can help mold a person.

The Lord gave me the perfect example just before I began writing this chapter. It came from the devotional from *Our Daily Bread*, for June 5, 2008, by Mark DeHaan. He told about a high school commencement speaker chosen for the occasion because of his success as the president of a large corporation. Yet in his speech he offered a most unusual wish for the graduates. He told them, "If I could have one hope for you as you go out into the world, it would be this: I hope you fail. I hope that you fail at something that is important to you." He went on to say how his own life had been one failure after another, until he learned to see failure as an effective teacher. The final thought of the devotional was, "Learn from your failures or you will fail to learn."

What a great message for all of us as we struggle against the many land mines and giants in our daily lives. It's a matter of attitude, response, and seeing our adversities from God's perspective. I personally learned a great lesson when I failed the North Carolina bar exam the first time around. Up until that time my life had been smooth and without flaw. To a certain extent, I thought I was invincible. Along with everybody else, I thought I was on top of the world and in charge. To borrow the words of William Ernest Henly in his poem "Invictus," I thought I was "the master of my fate" and the "captain of my soul." It took that traumatic failure to bring me to my knees and give me a humble spirit of dependency on the real Master of my fate and the true Captain of my soul.

After keying in this section on adversities, my good friend (and typist) Linda Murray told me of what her mother had written in her Bible years ago: "May there be enough clouds in your lifetime to make a lovely sunset."

Wishing for clouds? Most of us prefer sunshine over clouds any day. And yet the loveliest and most unforgettable sunsets require a setting of dark clouds to bring out the true beauty of such a picturesque scene. As hard as it may have been, Linda's mother had the insight and wisdom to wish for her daughter enough dark times to come into her life to achieve the overriding purpose of allowing her to learn many valuable lessons. She saw the advantages of adversity.

Here, summarized from the writings of Charles Stanley, are some thoughts that can help us discover the true benefits and advantages of enduring the pain of adversity. A whole new light is shed on our suffering and hardship when viewed from God's perspective.

- *Adversity is God's way of getting our attention.* Has He been the priority of your life, or have you ignored His will for your own? Your difficulty may be a signal that you need a priority change. Maybe it's time for self-examination.
- *Adversity is God's way of reminding us that He loves us.* His purpose is to protect us from completely destroying ourselves.
- *Adversity is God's way of conquering our pride.* Prosperity breeds forgetfulness. Success often breeds pride, which in turn leads to failure. "God is opposed to the proud, but gives grace to the humble" (1 Peter 5:5). Adversity has a way of stripping away our pride.
- *Adversity is God's way of reminding us of our weakness and our need for dependency on Him.* When our back is to the wall and there seems to be no way out, we suddenly recognize we are not sufficient in ourselves. We need the Lord. Through my weakness of failing the bar exam, I became strong through God's grace.
- *Adversity is God's way of demonstrating His faithfulness.* Our helpless state is God's opportunity to keep His promise to us. "The righteous

cry and the Lord hears, and delivers them out of all their troubles" (Psalm 34:17).

- *Adversity is God's way of preparing us to confront others.* We become more useful to God and others through our own suffering. We should view our trials as a profitable period of equipping us for better serving God and man.

- *Adversity is God's way of increasing our hatred of evil.* Our hardship is often of our own making. Whatever we sow, we will reap (Galatians 6:7). Heat purifies; hot water keeps one clean. Yesterday's adversity is strong motivation for today's obedience.

- *Adversity is God's tool for showing Him where we stand in our faith.* It is His most accurate barometer for faith. Do we doubt God? Do we thank Him for His faithfulness? Can we trust Him when He says He will never forsake us?

- *Adversity is God's tool for building godly, spiritual character into our lives.* Until we experience heartache, disappointment, and pain, we are not properly equipped for service (Romans 5:3). He uses adversity to mold and shape us. He doesn't bring it into our lives without purpose.

- *God's ultimate design is to conform us to the image and likeness of Jesus.* He has something in mind. God uses adversity only so long as it is needed. Once it has performed its function, He takes it away.

How Does God See Us?

Through adversity God is molding us into more mature children of His. When He looks at us during our struggles, what does He see? He sees a saint (a believer), sometimes struggling, sometimes falling, but justified, redeemed, forgiven, and reconciled to Him. He sees a saint full of His unconditional love, indwelt by His presence, sealed by the Holy Spirit of promise, whose name is written in the Lamb's Book of Life. He sees us on our way to heaven, with purpose and direction for our lives. He sees us in whom adversity can never take up permanent residence. When we learn and mature in the midst of adversity, God is pleased because He sees His purpose being fulfilled in us.

We are growing spiritually and becoming stronger in areas of weakness—and increasingly being conformed to the likeness of His Son, Jesus Christ, which thrills God. He wants to break us of the idea that we are self-sufficient. He made us for a loving, dependent relationship with Him, and He uses adversity to remind us of that fact.

Chapter 9

OBSERVATIONS MADE FROM MY
PLAYING THE GAME OF LIFE

As I continue my journey in playing the game of life, and as I find myself moving closer toward my time of graduation from the College of Life, let me make several observations. Hopefully they will provide readers with at least a small measure of helpful insight as they continue their own journey in playing the game. These observations come as a result of my being brought up in a church setting all my life. I have been blessed with many good friends and have generally been associated with good people from early childhood, on through my education experiences from grammar school to college and law school, and then to the rewarding experiences of law practice as well as community and church service.

Here are seven spiritual observations I've made from my journey in playing the game of life.

Observation #1: As a General Rule, No One Wants to
Talk about Sin. It Sounds Too Biblical.

Basically sin is anything that separates us from God. It has been defined as "falling short of the mark." It has also been defined as "the willful breaking of religious or moral laws." The Bible refers to sin as disobedience. Sin falls into two major categories: sin with a capital "S" and sin with a small "s."

Sin with a capital "S" is our sin nature. We are born into sin because we have the blood of Adam in us. In that respect everyone is a sinner, and we will continue to have that sin nature throughout our earthly existence unless we are born again and are given eternal life.

Sin with a small "s" represents the many sins of commission and omission that we commit on a daily basis. They can be either small sins or large sins, minor sins or major sins. However you describe them, "Sin" and "sins" separated us from God. We don't like to talk about being sinners, because it makes us feel guilty or sound too religious. Why does it make us feel guilty? Because we *are* guilty, and nobody wants to be judged that way.

Observation #2: As a General Rule, People, Including a Lot of "Good" Church People, Are Reluctant to Mention the Name "Jesus." It's too religious.

Have you ever noticed how a lot of folks, if they are in the right setting, will mention the name "God" rather freely? But even in the same setting, they feel uncomfortable to talk about or even say the name of "Jesus." It's going a little too far; it sounds too religious. Some church folks even find it a little awkward to conclude a prayer with, "In Jesus' name." And yet Jesus is at the very core of what and who Christianity is all about. He's what the Bible is all about. Everything in the Old Testament, from beginning to end, points ahead to the coming of Jesus. Everything in the New Testament points back to the two comings of Jesus: first as a baby in Bethlehem, second as the glorious King. As we've already said, "Christianity is not a religion, it's a relationship." It's having a personal relationship with God through His Son, Jesus the Christ.

Observation #3: A Lot of Church People Don't Want to Talk about "the Blood" or "the Blood of Jesus." It's Too Gory.

Some people even find it offensive to see a picture of the blood-stained body of Jesus hanging on a cross. Only occasionally do you see a halfway true picture of what His bloody, mangled body must have looked like as He hung suffering on the cross in indescribable pain and agony. In one sense, it's easy to understand how many would shy away from talking about the bloody, gory body of our Savior hanging shamefully and pitifully between two thieves. But on the other hand, His blood sacrifice was necessary for the redemption of the sins of the world. That's the very reason Jesus came from heaven to live on earth. He came to die, and to shed His blood for us so that those believing in Him might live. God's Word makes it clear: "Without the shedding of blood there is no forgiveness of sin" (Hebrews 9:22).

Observation #4: Many People Do Not Believe in a Literal Hell. If God Truly Loves Us as the Bible Says He Does, Why Would He Allow Anyone to End Up in What the Bible Calls Hell?

That kind of reasoning may appear to make sense, at least from the worldly or secular view. The only problem is that's not what the Bible teaches. Jesus talked a lot about heaven, but he talked even more about hell. The Bible refers to hell as an actual place of torment and damnation, and whoever goes there will live in an eternal state of separation from God. Some people reason that when their earthly existence is over, that's it. Life is all over. They believe they will not know anything and will not be aware of their surroundings. This is contrary to biblical teaching, for they will indeed experience an eternal existence of torment and suffering (to put it mildly). This eternal existence is reserved for those who choose to play the game of death rather than the game of life. The sad thing is it will last forever—not for just a hundred years, or a thousand years, but forever and ever and ever! God tells us through His Word that a person's soul will never die. We will live eternally in one of two places: either in heaven with God, or in hell separated from God.

Observation #5: Although Most All Church People Believe in the Bible, Many Don't Believe It Is All True in Its Entirety. Most of It May Be True, but Certainly Not All of It.

Some of these "unbelievers" in the inerrancy of the Bible can stretch their belief system enough to accept some of the miracles of Jesus as "maybe being true." But when it comes to some of the Old Testament miracles of the parting

of the Red Sea, the flood, Jonah being swallowed by a great fish, and the
taking of Elijah into heaven "by a whirlwind," that's just too much and too
far-fetched. Human reasoning says it can't be done. But to believe in the inerrancy of the Bible is ultimately a matter of faith. You either believe what the
Word of God says about itself or you don't. You either believe the testimony
of Jesus Christ regarding the Word of God or you don't. The Bible itself tells
us how it was written: "All Scripture is inspired by God" (2 Timothy 3:16).
Second Peter 1:27 adds to our understanding by telling us, "Holy men of God
spoke as they were moved by the Holy Spirit." Here God is telling us that the
Holy Spirit carried men along, moving them and guiding them as they wrote
in their own words what God wanted them to say. I believe that every part of
the Bible is inspired by God and that it does not merely contain the words of
God, but it truly is God's Word. When you hold the Bible in your hand, you
are actually holding the Word of God.

Observation #6: A Lot of "Good People" Find It Hard to Believe That Jesus Is the Only Way to Heaven. They Reason That All the Other Religions Can't Be Wrong.

Here's where a number of my friends, both Christian and non-Christian, will
disagree with me. They reason that I'm being too narrow-minded and even
close-minded to claim that Jesus is the only way to have peace with God and
eternal life with Him. But my answer is, if Jesus is not the only way, who is
or what is? Is it Buddha, Confucius, or Allah? Is it through Shintoism, Hinduism, or some of the other many Eastern religions? Is it by adding up your
good deeds and working your way up the ladder toward heaven? Are you
hoping that you will somehow get enough points to gain God's favor and win
His approval to qualify you for entrance into His heavenly kingdom? The
logical questions for all of us seeking the truth are simply these: What is the
basis for your belief? What is at the foundation for your claim? Are you basing
it all merely on what you believe to be true and what sounds right? Are you
basing your eternal existence on a tradition or the most popular prevailing
view, or what some respected friend has told you?

It's amazing how our worldly thinking, particularly over the last fifty years, has deteriorated to the point where it is in vogue to think there are no absolutes. Modern thought would tell us there is no absolute truth. You can believe what you want to. As long as most people or at least a majority of the people believe it, it must be true. They can't all be wrong. In my own mind I am convinced that absolute truth does exist. There is a right, and there is a wrong. Granted there are allowances for gray areas for certain things that are considered nonessential or unimportant. In these areas differing opinions are acceptable. On the other hand, certain fundamental, basic things in life leave no room for personal opinion, or what may seem to be right. In those cases it's either black or white, either right or wrong. That two plus two is four is inarguable. It's always been four—this year, last year, last century, or the fifteenth century. Liquid water is wet. It's always been wet, and it always will be wet. These are established, God-given facts that have been true from the beginning of time.

So it is with the door to heaven. Since His sacrificial death on the cross and miraculous resurrection from the grave, Jesus has been and continues to be God's provision for eternal life in heaven. There is no room for argument—that is, if the Bible is true and without error. And that's the key to it all: *if* the Bible is true. It's either true or not true. If the Bible is not true in its entirety, then any one error in the biblical record opens the door to other errors. How do we know what's true and what's not true? Jesus said, "I am the Way, the Truth, and the Life; no one comes to the Father, but through me." (John 14:6). If that statement is not true, then Jesus was a liar. If He lied about that, He obviously would lie about other things.

Returning to the original question, if you do not believe that Jesus is the only way, I would merely ask this one question: what is the basis for your belief that He is not the only way? I'm basing my belief on the Bible. If the Bible is not true, then I'm wrong, and my whole belief system is out of whack. In fact, my whole life would be for naught, for I am basing both my earthly existence as well as my eternal existence on the truth of God's Word, the Bible. Just because some may not believe it does not keep it from being the eternal truth of the ages. The Bible is a unique book. It was written over a period of some fifteen hundred years with some forty different authors, yet it is one book without contradictions in what it says.

Is Jesus Really the Only Way? What Do Others Say?

I have given you what God says in His Word, that we only have eternal life through Jesus. There is no other way. But let's look at what others claim.

TV star Oprah Winfrey recently declared on her Web site, "I am a free-thinking Christian." She went on to say, "I am a Christian who thinks there are many more paths to God than Christianity." Obviously she doesn't believe God and His Word. She has also promoted New Age teacher Eckhart Tolle's book, *A New Earth*, the best-selling paperback that promotes dangerous New Age doctrine sharply at odds with biblical Christianity. The book is a fusion of Eastern mysticism—especially Buddhism and Hinduism—and the Bible, which it often misinterprets. This mixture is deadly, alluring and deceptively dangerous in its ability to divert people away from a true relationship with God.

Tolle, for instance, describes sin as a misunderstood and misinterpreted concept, and not the violation of God's moral law. For him, sin means "to miss the point of human existence." Obviously, he along with Oprah either hasn't read the Bible, or if he has he doesn't believe it. Dr. Robert Jeffress, senior pastor of First Baptist Church in Dallas, Texas, says that, "Eckhart Tolle completely twists the definition of sin. Tolle says sin is missing the point of life, or sin is failing to realize our God connectiveness. But the Bible says in Romans 3:23 that sin is missing God's standard, 'For all have sinned and come short of the glory of God.'" In general, Tolle calls on readers to transcend their ego-based lives to awaken to a "new state of consciousness." In this "awaking," Tolle asserts, world conflict and suffering can end. He also writes that heaven "is not a location, but refers to the inner realm of consciousness." He says that is what Jesus really meant in His teachings. To the contrary, Jesus said in John 14 that heaven is a place. He said, "I am going to prepare a place for you." Note that the Greek word for "place" is *topon*, which means geographical location.

Oprah Winfrey and Eckhart Tolle are modern-day examples of how "free-thinking" Christians can stray from the truth of God's Word to pursue their own way of thinking rather than stick to the plumb line of truth as revealed in the Bible. Times and philosophical thinking change. Truth does not.

Observation #7: Many "Good" Church People as Well as "Good" Nonchurch People Have Never Experienced Their Salvation through Jesus Christ.

This is not to judge anyone. I am merely stating what I believe to be a fact based on what I have observed. I have even heard several preachers say they preached in church for ten, fifteen, and in one case twenty years without knowing Jesus as his personal Savior. They had preached about Jesus, but did not know Jesus on a personal basis. They had never personally prayed the sinner's prayer. Let me give you a couple of examples, one of which turned out good, the other not so good:

- Some years ago I went to the hospital to visit a former Sunday school teacher of mine. She was on her deathbed. While talking to her I discovered that she was not sure she was going to heaven when she died. She had taught about the "good things" of the Christian life, but never taught the most essential thing about God's grace and the forgiveness of sins through the death of Jesus on the cross. This opened the door for me to explain to her that the Bible makes it clear that she can know for sure she is going to heaven. She doesn't have to think so. She can know so. I then explained it's a matter of believing on the Lord Jesus Christ. Romans 10:9 tells us "that if you confess with your mouth, 'Jesus is Lord,' and believe in your heart that God raised Him from the dead, you will be saved." Although it's been probably twenty-five or thirty years ago, I remember telling her of the apostle John's words when he said, "He who has the Son has life. He who does not have the Son does not have life. I write these things to you who believe in the name of the Son of God so that you may know that you have eternal life" (1 John 5:12–13). Before my leaving her bedside, she was led to trust Jesus as her Savior. She also joyously acknowledged that she knew for sure she was going to heaven when she died. I could tell in her eyes that she was relieved and felt good about her future existence. Now she was at peace, for she was confidently looking forward to being in the eternal presence of her Lord and Savior. I think it was about two weeks later she died. What a difference it made for her to know the truth!

- I know of a lot of other church people who are not sure about their salvation. They say in effect, "Well, I hope so. I hope I'm going to heaven when I die." I even heard a retired preacher tell a group in church that he had no way of knowing for sure he would end up in heaven. In fact, his comment was, "I won't know until I get there." He said it would be assuming too much to say he knew for sure he's going to heaven. He believed that God would judge him on the way he lived his life. He said he had been a longtime member and minister of the church, and felt that he had done a pretty good job in serving his congregation. After further inquiry he said he believed God would look at his life as a whole, and if his good deeds outweighed his bad deeds he would be granted entrance into heaven. He said he felt pretty good about his chances, but there was no way he could be sure. He obviously was just expressing his personal opinion based on what sounded logical and reasonable to him. Even though he professed to be a minister of the gospel, it was also obvious he knew nothing about what the Bible says over and over again: that we are saved only by God's grace, and not by our good works. The Bible makes it clear that you can never do enough good deeds to earn your way into heaven. I pointed out several Scriptures to show that we are saved by the free gift of God's grace (through His Son) and not by our good works. But nothing I said could change his way of thinking. I was reminded of 1 Corinthians 1:18: "For the message of the cross is foolishness to those who are perishing." It's not up to me to judge anyone, but I can't help but wonder where his soul is today. It saddens me to realize that countless other church people and good people fall in the same category. I understand this minister died a year or so later. Assuming he never "saw the light," one can't help but see the difference in how this minister went to his grave, as contrasted with my former Sunday school teacher after the light of God's truth was revealed to her.

Chapter 10

A REVIEW: SEEING THE BIG PICTURE,
SUMMING UP THE GAME OF LIFE, AND
PASSING IT ON TO OTHERS

So what have we learned as we have been playing the game of life? As we have faced the twelve giants throughout our career at the College of Life, what can we pass on to the younger players who might benefit from our experience?

Have you ever noticed that from time to time some of the former Tar Heel basketball stars will come back and scrimmage half court with those coming up through the ranks? NBA greats Michael Jordan, Jerry Stackhouse, Sean May, and Raymond Felton have all acted as mentors for the young rising stars. I'm certainly no star player, but at the same time, I've learned some things from merely being a longtime participant that might be of help for the younger players.

One of the basic things I've learned personally, and which I am still trying to put into regular practice, is to look at my trials and adversities from God's perspective. He knows the whole story of my life from beginning to end. He knew from the day I was born what challenges I would face that would bring me to this point in my life, and He knows what lies before me and what giants I will face in the future. My life is all is in His hands. He knows exactly the time and place my earthly existence will end, and when my eternal existence with Him will begin. He knows the big picture of my life. He has been my Coach all these years, and I feel that He, as the Inventor of "the game," has taught me many valuable lessons as a player.

So what does He want me to pass on to you, the reader? Keep in mind I'm still trying to learn. I'm still trying to follow His instructions and be led by the greatest of all coaches: the Sovereign God of the Universe.

By way of review, here are ten of the basic things I've learned about the game of life.

1. ***You begin playing the game of life by accepting Jesus as your Lord and Savior.*** Only through Him can you have eternal life and be qualified to play the game of life. If you're not playing the game of life, you're automatically playing the game of death. These are the only two spiritual games available to us as we go through our earthly existence.

2. ***The game of life is a spiritual game, not a physical game.*** We play our opponents on spiritual, not physical battlefields. "For our struggle is not against flesh and blood, but against the rulers, against the powers, against the world forces of this darkness, against the spiritual forces of wickedness in the heavenly place" (Ephesians 6:12).

3. ***Our coach is the Sovereign God of the Universe.*** As the inventor of the game, He knows every aspect of how it should be played. He has provided us the Rule Book, which is known as His Word or the Bible. By reading and studying it on a daily basis we become familiar with the general rules and His style of play. A second way to keep in touch with our Coach is through what is commonly known as prayer. He is never too busy to talk to His players. He makes Himself available to us twenty-four hours a day, seven days a week. He never sleeps. He wants us to be the best players we can be.

4. ***Our Coach's highest priority for His players is that we know Him personally and have an intimate relationship with Him.*** The more intimate we are with our Coach, the greater the impact our lives will have as players of the game of life.

5. ***Our Coach's number-one purpose for all His players is that we be conformed to the image and likeness of His Son.*** This is called "sanctification"

and is a lifelong process. Jesus was the perfect example, the perfect player of the game of life. His number-one purpose on earth was to do the will of His Father. It will take a lifetime of playing at the College of Life for our Coach to fulfill His purpose for each of His players. On graduation day, also known as Commencement Day, we will indeed be like Jesus. We will be holy and perfect as we enter His heavenly kingdom and begin our external existence in His holy presence.

6. ***Our game opponents are all led by the same coach, known commonly as Satan or the devil.*** His number-one purpose is to discourage, defeat, and destroy all of us who oppose him. He will use every trick of his trade to fulfill his purpose. He is the great deceiver and a murderer. As Paul advised us in 1 Peter 5:8, "Be sober, be vigilant, because your adversary the devil walks about like a roaring lion, seeking whom he may devour."

7. ***We need to get in shape to compete against the fierce opposition.*** We've got to be ready to compete. Our number-one weapon is preparation, and our number-one tactic is time. We have to spend sufficient quality time in reading and understanding our Coach's Rule Book. Not only do we need a thorough understanding of the rules of the game, it is vital that we get a clear understanding of what our Coach expects of us. He wants us to win, and we can win every game if we know and follow our Coach's instructions. It won't be easy. There'll be many ups and downs. We may fall behind in the score, but by keeping our eyes focused on our Coach, we will eventually emerge victorious at the end of the game. Most importantly we will win the crown of life upon graduating from the College of Life. On that glorious day we will make the transition from the drudgery of our earthly existence to the bliss of our heavenly existence. Only then will we truly understand that it was worth it all. Paul emphasized the point beautifully when he said, "For I consider that the sufferings of this present time are not worthy to be compared with the glory which shall be revealed in us" (Romans 8:18). The word "consider" means "to compute or calculate." Dennis Fisher said, "When eternity is brought into our calculation of a problem, future glory overshadows current pain."

8. ***The key to victory over our twelve adversary giants is having the right response to the challenge.*** The giants themselves can't hurt you. The right response to each adversary brings victory. The right response involves the right attitude, which means looking at each adversary from God's perspective. God allows adversity in our lives for a good purpose, mainly to develop godly character. He wants to break us down and strip away our self-dependency and cause us to depend on Him as our heavenly Father. In essence we find victory in surrender. When we are weak in our own power, we become strong in His grace. Disappointments are inevitable. Discouragement and shrinking back in fear is a choice. We don't have to choose to be afraid. God has told us many times in His Word, "Fear not" and "Do not be discouraged for I am with you."

9. ***There are many mysteries in this life, many things we don't understand. We're not supposed to understand everything.*** The good news is, in a world of mystery, it's a comfort to know the God who knows all things. He knows the answer to every mystery of life. The doctrine of omniscience tells us that God knows all things, which has important implications for our spiritual lives, especially when we realize that His omniscience includes knowledge of all our needs—our ordinary needs as well as those seemingly impossible-to-handle needs. In the marvelous work of salvation and sanctification, God knew us before the foundation of the world: "For whom He foreknew, He also predestined to be conformed to the image of His Son, that He might be the first born among many brethren" (Romans 8:29). Acts 15:18 also tells us, "Known to God from eternity are all His works."

So often we struggle in trying to figure life out. We face many events and circumstances that baffle us. We're reminded of London's legendary detective Sherlock Holmes and his investigative genius as he routinely assessed seemingly random clues to solve a mystery. Baffled by Holmes's uncanny brilliance, his sidekick, Dr. Watson, would ask for an explanation, to which Holmes would glibly respond, "Elementary!" and then proceed to unfold the solution. The answers to the mysteries of life are elementary for the Sovereign God of the Universe. "'For My thoughts are not your thoughts nor are your ways My ways,' says the Lord. 'For as the heavens are higher than the earth so are My ways higher than your ways and My thoughts than your thoughts'" (Isaiah 55:8–9).

10. ***Growing old is a blessing when you're close to God.*** Americans spend more than $20 billion annually on various antiaging products that claim to cure baldness, remove wrinkles, build muscles, and renew the power of youth. We've been told by leading researchers that there is absolutely no scientific proof that any commercially available product will stop or reverse aging. We might be able to slow down the inevitable, but we can't stop it. But the promise is there of a spiritual vitality that defies the ravages of time. Isaiah used the eagle as the symbol of freedom and endurance, held aloft by a source of power outside itself. As we put our hope and trust in the Lord, we are carried along by His strength and not our own. The Psalmist said that the Lord nourishes us so that our "youth is renewed like the eagle's" (Psalm 103:5).

Chapter 11

THE FINAL CHAPTER—MISSION ACCOMPLISHED: GRADUATION FROM THE COLLEGE OF LIFE

In the physical world graduation day is often referred to as Commencement Day, because it signifies the commencement or beginning of a new life. We've completed our college days and are now ready to begin our work life. We've been studying and preparing ourselves all these years. Now it's time to put all that learning to good use and go out into the workforce and make a living. The same is true in the spiritual world and the College of Life. For those who genuinely made the conscious decision during their earthly existence to accept Jesus Christ as their Savior, they have been living as a Christian, at least "in position." Someone has referred to our position as being our Christian status as a human being. As we've previously pointed out, our position is one of a Christian, even though in practice we are far from it. We fall short every day, for many times we don't act like a Christian. We don't always live up to who we are in Christ.

The good news is that we are being sanctified. Our heavenly Father is daily conforming us to the image and likeness of His Son. For some of us it is a very slow process; for others the process is much faster. But if we are truly born-again Christians, the good news is that we are at least heading in the right direction. We are qualified and ready for Commencement Day!

How sad to observe that some people, even some Christians, live their lives thinking only of the here and now, without ever looking ahead to the end of their lives. It is as if we avoid considering our end for fear that our thinking about it will bring it to pass. In my law practice I've had people come in to discuss preparing their wills. They say they've put it off as long as they can, because they just don't want to talk about dying. They look at it as a morbid subject. On the other hand, many others are able to talk openly and freely about it. They are realistic in their thinking. Even though they may be sick and their prognosis is discouraging, they are upbeat, and it is easy to tell from their general demeanor that they know where they're going when they die. They know for sure they're going to make the transition into God's heavenly kingdom in the twinkling of an eye, when they take their last breath on earth.

Completing the Course: Finishing Strong

As Christians we will finish the race, as far as salvation is concerned, but there's still a danger we may not finish strong. What does finishing strong mean? It has a lot to do with our thought process and attitude as we look to the future and realize our time on earth is short. It has everything to do with knowing the truth as revealed in God's Word: "And you shall know the truth, and the truth shall make you free" (John 8:32). As a general rule, our thinking becomes more realistic as we age. As we approach and surpass our life expectancy according to the actuarial tables, we begin to realize the truth. We reason, *At best I can't have but a few more years left—whether it's one, five, ten, or fifteen years at the max.* When you turn seventy-five and eighty, such thinking definitely becomes a part of your mind-set. How should we live out our last few years?

From our Bible study on heaven, we learned that what we think about has a great deal to do with how we live on earth. Heaven is like an anchor to which we are tied, and it is pulling us through the present to the future. Heaven will definitely not be boring. As a believer we will have a brand-new body suited for heavenly living. It will be like Jesus' body as witnessed by His disciples during the forty days between His resurrection and ascension. At the judgment seat of Christ we will be judged on how we lived our lives on earth. "For we must all appear before the judgment seat of Christ, that each may receive the things done in the body, according to what he has done, whether good or bad" (2 Corinthians 5:10). This will be the time when we will be rewarded for our service to the Lord in our Christian experience. Knowing this should motivate us to finish strong by living out our last days in serving the Lord. This is a matter of faithfulness on the part of those already saved.

The *judgment seat of Christ* is reserved for Christians only. The Bible also refers to the **great white throne of judgment** which is reserved for unbelievers, those who have not been saved from their sins (see Revelation 20:11ff.). On that dreadful Day of Judgment, those refusing to accept Jesus as Savior will be cast into the lake of fire where there will be "weeping and gnashing of teeth," eternally separated from God. It may be hard for some to believe this and accept it as true, but that's what the Bible says, and I believe it.

Finishing Strong Implies Endurance

James 1:12 states, "Blessed is the man who endures trial." The Lord will indeed bless those who persevere when battling with the twelve giants that we all face from time to time. No one escapes those challenges. Satan is constantly placing land mines in our path. They are inescapable. As we've already learned, it's how we respond to the land mines that sets the stage for victory. The right attitude makes the difference, but the bottom line is endurance. Don't give up! When His disciples grew discouraged in the midst of a storm, Jesus told them, "It is I, don't be afraid." He is telling all believers not to be afraid as we struggle to persevere in the midst of trials. As Paul told the Philippian believers, "And my God shall supply all your needs according to His riches in glory by Jesus Christ" (Philippians 4:19). Knowing the truth of God's Word gives us encouragement to endure to the end. Our final reward will be more than worth it.

To Finish Strong, We Need to Put on the Full Armor of God

In Ephesians 6:10–18, the apostle Paul zeroes in on our struggles and identifies the various articles of armor each Christian needs to put on to assure us of victory over the enemy:

Finally, be strong in the Lord and in the strength of His might. Put on the full armor of God, that you may be able to stand firm against the schemes of the devil. For our struggle is not against flesh and blood, but against the rulers, against the powers, against the world forces of this darkness, against the spiritual forces of wickedness in the heavenly places. Therefore take up the full armor of God, that you may be able to resist in the evil day, and having done everything, to stand firm. Stand firm therefore, having girded your loins with truth, and having put on the breastplate of righteousness, and having shod your feet with the preparation of the Gospel of Peace. In addition to all, taking up the shield of faith with which you will be able to extinguish all the flaming missiles of the evil one and take the helmet of salvation and the Sword of the Spirit, which is the Word of God. With all prayer and petition pray at all times in the Spirit, and with this in view, be on the alert with all perseverance and petition for all the saints.

Notice that Paul identifies six items in our "armor of God":

The belt of truth
The breastplate of righteousness
The shoes of the preparation of the gospel of peace
The shield of faith
The helmet of salvation
The sword of the Spirit, which is the Word of God

Notice also that the first five items are defensive in nature, and that the only offensive weapon is the sword of the Spirit, which is the Word of God. We must stay in the Word if we are to properly prepare ourselves to be victorious over the enemy. The more we know the Coach's rules and are obedient to them, the better prepared we are to finish strong as we look toward graduation from the College of Life.

It should also be noted that Paul focuses on prayer as the foundation fuel that powers all aspects of our spiritual armor. Prayer makes us go as Christians. Without prayer we simply cannot maintain the power and energy to be victorious in the spiritual battle known as the Christian life. It is no more possible to live the Christian life without prayer than it is to run a gasoline engine on diesel fuel. Lack of prayer is often considered the cause of so many casualties in Christian spiritual warfare. We're often tempted to try all sorts of substitutes to make us go, but in the end, prayer—as well as staying in the Word—provides the fuel for the Christian life. Without constant prayer we will not finish strong.

Finishing Strong Requires Constant Prayer

THE WARRIOR'S PRAYER

Heavenly Father,
Your warrior prepares for battle.
Today I claim victory over Satan by putting on
The whole armor of God!
I put on the girdle of truth!
May I stand firm in the truth of Your Word
So I will not be a victim of Satan's lies.

I put on the breastplate of righteousness!
May it guard my heart from evil
So I will remain pure and holy,
Protected under the blood of Jesus Christ.

I put on the shoes of peace!
May I stand firm in the good news of the gospel
So Your peace will shine through me
And be a light to all I encounter.

I take the shield of faith!
May I be ready for Satan's fiery darts of
Doubt, Denial, and Deceit
So I will not be vulnerable to spiritual defeat.

I put on the helmet of salvation!
May I keep my mind focused on you
So Satan will not have a stronghold on my
thoughts.

I take the sword of the Spirit!
May the two-edged sword of your word
Be ready in my hands
So I can expose the tempting words of Satan.

By faith your warrior has put on
The whole armor of God!
I am prepared to live this day in spiritual victory!
Amen.

(Handout received from David Jeremiah)

What Is It Like to "Make the Transition"?

In his later years my father often talked about "making the transition." He was referring to what the world calls death, but what he knew to be the passing of his soul and spirit from his earthly existence to his eternal heavenly life with his Maker. When he was diagnosed with cancer in April 1968 he accepted the fact that his time would probably be short. That didn't mean that he and all the family didn't pray for healing, because we did. But it meant that he was ready for whatever outcome came his way. If the Lord healed him, he would remain here on earth for a while longer to enjoy his life of service to the Lord and be a witness to others. On the other hand, if the Lord called him home, he would go to be with Jesus and live eternally with Him. That's where he always wanted to be, so he couldn't lose, no matter if he lived or died. He was able to identify with Paul when he said:

> For I fully expect and hope that I will never be ashamed, but I will continue to be bold for Christ, as I have been in the past. And I trust that my life will bring honor to Christ, whether I live or die. For me, living means living for Christ, and dying is even better. But if I live, I can do more fruitful work for Christ. So I really don't know which is better. I'm torn between two desires; I long to go and be with Christ, which would be far better for me. But for your sakes, it is better that I continue to live (Philippians 1:20–24).

The footnote in Margaret's New Living Translation of her *Life Application Study Bible* gives us keen insight as we apply Daddy's experience to our own lives:

> To those who don't believe in God, life on earth is all there is, and so it is natural for them to strive for the world's values: money, popularity, power, pleasure, and prestige. For Paul, however, to live meant to develop eternal values and to tell others about Christ, who alone could help them see life from an eternal perspective. Paul's whole purpose in life was to speak out boldly for Christ and to become more like him. Thus, Paul could confidently say that dying would be even better than living, because in death he would be removed from worldly troubles, and he would see Christ face to face (John 3:2–3). If you're not ready to die, then you're not ready to live. Make certain of your eternal destiny; then you will be free to serve—devoting your life to what really counts, without fear of death.

What a statement that is for you and me to ponder!

Daddy told all the family on more than one occasion, "Don't cry over my dead body, because that won't be me. I'll be gone. I'll be with Jesus, so I want you to sing 'Glory Hallelujah.'" And so we did just that. Even though we went through a time of grieving, it was nevertheless a time of rejoicing, because we knew the truth, and he had prepared us for that eventuality. We knew the meaning of "making the transition." All Christians should have the mind-set of Paul when he said, "We are confident, yes, well pleased rather to be absent from the body and to be present with the Lord" (2 Corinthians 5:8).

I am reminded of the following beautiful description of dying by Henry VanDyke in his "Parable of Immortality":

I am standing upon the seashore.
A ship at my side spreads her white sails to the morning breeze
and starts for the blue ocean.
She is an object of beauty and strength,
and I stand and watch her until at last she hangs
like a speck of white cloud
just where the sea and sky come down to mingle with each other.
Then someone at my side says,
"There she goes!"
Gone where?
Gone from my sight . . . that is all.
She is just as large in mast and hull and spar
as she was when she left my side
and just as able to bear her load of living freight
to the place of destination.
Her diminished size is in me, not in her.
And just at the moment
when someone at my side says,
"There she goes!"
there are other eyes watching her coming . . .
and other voices ready to take up the glad shouts . . .
"Here she comes!"

That's a good description of what it means to make the transition—from this world to the next. Even more comforting for the loved ones of a believer who dies are the words of the apostle Paul: "If our earthly house, this tent, is destroyed, we have a building from God a house not made with hands, external in the heavens" (2 Corinthians 5:1). We can rejoice in our sorrow knowing our departed loved ones are now present with the Lord. To the Christian, death is a time of rejoicing in the midst of sad loss. Because Christ lives, death is not tragedy, but triumph, and as the familiar hymn says, "Because He lives I can face tomorrow!"

Chapter 12

THE DEGREE OF DOCTOR OF PHILOSOPHY IN HOMEMAKING IS AWARDED TO ELIZABETH ANN SEIPP PERRY FROM THE COLLEGE OF LIFE

October 14, 1962, was a special day in the life of the Ely J. Perry family. That marked the fortieth wedding anniversary of my mother and father. The celebration dinner took place at the Kinston Country Club, when at the appropriate time my mother was surprised in a most unique way. All the family was there, including Mother and Daddy; my brother Warren and his wife Barbara and their four children, Wes, Betty Blaine, Jimbo, and Ashely; also my brother Ely Jr. and his wife, Barbara Ruth, along with their only child at the time, daughter Ruth E. I was not married until the following March, so I was there as a bachelor. I was, however, far enough along in my courtship of Margaret that I invited her to share in this special occasion. Then there were a whole bunch of cousins and aunts and uncles. We had a big crowd. After a delightful dinner Daddy quieted the group and made his announcement. He wanted to recognize and pay tribute to "Elizabeth" in a special way. He went on to relate many kind and thoughtful remarks about his dear wife of forty years. He told us how much he had loved her all those years, and that she was prettier now than she had ever been. In fact, he told the crowd, as he had told us three boys many times as we were growing up, that he loved her even more now than when he first met her. He then reached under the table and pulled out a large picture frame. As he showed it to the anxious group, all eyes were

Daddy, age 52   *Mother, age 50*

glued not only on Daddy but also on Mother. We were all spellbound. What was he up to? Then he said he wanted to read what he prepared. I'm not sure if anyone else knew anything about what he was about to read, but he had told me how he was inspired to honor Mother and wanted to know if I had any suggestions or input. He had spent many long hours in preparing the wording of what he had framed, front and back.

On the front was the degree of "Doctor of Philosophy in Homemaking" which he designed himself. He called upon his nephew and my cousin, Jack Carey, to draft the design at Daddy's instruction. Jack was an architect and did a good job in sketching a small semblance of our home at 908 West Road. Beneath the home were the Latin words *Amor Omnia Bincit*, the translation of which is "Love Conquers All." On the left side of the house were a crown and a cross. On the right side were his office and desk, all representing God, home, and work. These three sketches were shown beneath the arched Old English lettering of "The College of Life." It really looked like a true-to-life diploma. In the lower left-hand corner was a seal with the circular words "The Great Seal of the Ely J. Perry Family" and the date 1922. In the center of the seal was the formation of a cross with the word "GOD" intersecting vertically and horizontally. Horizontally the word "WORKS" was on the left and "HOPE" on the right. Inside the vertical part of the cross were the words "LOVE" at the top and "FAITH" at the bottom. Daddy supplied the wording, and Jack drafted the artwork. It truly made a unique presentation.

On the back side of the frame was the citation Daddy had so meticulously prepared. He spent countless hours composing just the right wording to express his love, devotion, and appreciation for his sweetheart of over forty years.

Their fortieth anniversary occasion was only one of many highlights of the exemplary married life of my wonderful parents. I, along with my brothers Warren and Ely Jr., were blessed beyond measure to grow up in a home where love and understanding were displayed on a daily basis by both word and example. Daddy was a great role model and mentor after whom we boys could pattern our own marriages. Mother's loving and gracious response to Daddy, being the head of the household, was equally exemplary. The Lord was good to us (to say the least), and I will always be grateful. The examples set by Mother and Daddy were a splendid model of God's grace and mercy—certainly much more than we deserved!

Dan with Mother, age 80

The Father, Children, & Grandchildren
of the
Ely J. Perry Family
in
The College of Life

Amor Omnia Vincit

To all to whom these presents shall come
Greeting
Be It Known That

Elizabeth Ann Seipp Perry

having faithfully and unselfishly served for these Forty years as sweetheart, wife, mother, homemaker and Queen of the Ely J. Perry Kingdom in The College of Life and having constantly displayed during that time the highest ideals and most worthy qualities pursuant to her role in said family

and

having in every respect completed and fulfilled the requirements for the degree of

Doctor of Philosophy in Homemaking

has accordingly been admitted to all the rights, honors, and privileges appertaining to that degree.

In witness whereof the Great Seal of the Ely J. Perry Family and signatures of the duly authorized members thereof are affixed to this diploma.

Given at Kinston in the State of North Carolina this 14th day of October in the year of Our Lord nineteen hundred and sixty-two upon the Fortieth anniversary of the marriage of Elizabeth Ann Seipp and Ely Jackson Perry.

Ely J. Perry
Father

Warren S. Perry
Son

Barbara S. Perry
Daughter-in-Law

Warren S. Perry Jr.
Grandson

Elizabeth Blaine Perry
Granddaughter

James S. Perry
Grandson

Ashely A. B. [X] Perry
her Mark — Granddaughter

Ely J. Perry, Jr.
Son

Barbara Ruth Perry
Daughter-in-Law

Ruth Elizabeth [X] Perry
her Mark — Granddaughter

Dan E. Perry
Son

The Great Seal of The Ely J. Perry Family
19 22
LOVE GOD HOPE — WORKS GOD — FAITH

CITATION

ELIZABETH ANN SEIPP PERRY

FOR

DOCTOR OF PHILOSOPHY IN HOMEMAKING

IN THE COLLEGE OF LIFE

For being my sweetheart since first we met in August, 1920, and danced to the tune of "Love Nest"; for giving me a wonderful courtship for over twenty-six months, during which time you wrote more letters than there were days in the year; for becoming my beautiful bride on October 14, 1922, and during these forty succeeding years for being a constant inspiration and joy to live with;

For your patience and understanding throughout those first years when adjustments were necessary; for bearing our three sons, taking good care of them, loving them, training them, and leading them into the paths that gave them good bodies, minds, and souls, with a love and reverence for God and a love and respect for their fellowman; for going with us to Sunday School and Church; for your teaching in the Sunday School for many years and always encouraging our spiritual development;

For being a good listener when my burdens are heavy; for always being at my side, understanding, loving, and smiling and seeing the bright side in defeat and rejoicing in victory; for always inspiring me to nobler things, and helping to achieve our common goals; for bringing good books from the library and keeping the best spiritual pamphlets and books on my bedside table for me to read and for having me to read them to you; for instinctively anticipating my every need;

For being a wonderful cook, housekeeper, and provider of all the little essentials in the household to help make home the place where we are always glad to return to after working all day; for being an unselfish, loving, and inspiring mother, first to our three boys, and then to our two daughters-in-law, and then to our grandchildren; for getting up early when you so like to sleep late; for fixing good, wholesome meals, and at times when it is necessary for me to leave before daybreak, for never letting me go without a good breakfast, and on each overnight trip away from you for always having a love note in my pajama pocket; for meeting me at the door with a smile and a welcome kiss; for being economical and a good buyer, always getting the most out of what you spend;

For taking time out to play gin rummy with me, where each of us work hard to win but rejoice when the other is the winner; for always being neat, beautiful, and loving, with a smile that comes from the heart, and making me truly proud to introduce you to my friends;

For taking care of me in sickness and in health, and for watching my diet even though I grumble about not being able to eat what I want;

For always being ready on short notice to go on a trip and for being a good traveler and companion who is always enjoyed on every trip, helping to look after details and checking things to see that they are right; for helping me share our travel experiences with others;

For your natural artistic and decorative ability in adding beauty and grace to the home; for saving all kinds of household effects and then knowing where to find them; for being a wonderful housekeeper and for your good taste in selecting furniture, pictures, and bric-a-brac that have combined to make a beautiful house at 908 West Road which, crowned with love, has made for me the perfect home.

All of these things and countless other little, but wonderful, things too numerous to mention here, have gone into the everyday living which has made life wonderful, for you have truly been an inspiration to me, to all the children, and to all who know you, and, as such, you are the Queen of the Ely J. Perry Kingdom.

For all these contributions in the art of living we are happy and proud to present you with this degree of Doctor of Philosophy in Homemaking from the College of Life.

THE COLLEGE OF LIFE IN THE
ELY J. PERRY KINGDOM

Ely J. Perry
Headmaster

This October 14th., A. D., 1962.

Chapter 13

A TIME TO REFLECT AND DECIDE

At the conclusion of my first book, *More Than I Deserve*, I had originally planned the last section to be called "Postlude—A Challenge to the Reader: A Penetrating Question." Upon deeper reflection at the time and after running it by Margaret, we both decided the timing was wrong, that it would be a little too heavy for the reader at that point. We thought maybe those reading about the life of Dan Perry would think I had become too much of a fanatic in my old age. In the book I had talked about my recollections and memories from my birth to the present. I had talked about my search for truth and spiritual growth, and I had listed twenty-one lessons I had learned during my journey through this life. I also emphasized that only through Jesus Christ can we truly know the fullness of God and His unconditional, all-encompassing love for all mankind. According to the Bible, only through Jesus can we get to heaven when our earthly existence is over. That's what God's Word says. That's what Jesus Himself said as recorded by the apostle John who heard Him say, "I am the Way, the Truth, and the Life; no one comes to the Father, but through me" (John 14:6).

I really felt that the Lord led me not to mention the postlude in *More Than I Deserve*, but now as I come to the end of my writing *The Game of Life*, I feel the time is now right to include it. Maybe just one person (hopefully more) will see the need to receive Christ as Lord and Savior. We have talked about the fact that during our earthly existence, we must make a choice. We can either play the game of death or the game of life. You must play one or the other. You can't play both at the same time. If you don't accept Christ before you leave this earth, you automatically play the game of death. This leads to everlasting death, or eternal separation from God, which the Bible calls "hell." By making the conscious decision to accept Christ's invitation to play the game of life, we gain eternal life and entrance into heaven. It's a simple decision, but the gravity of that decision determines our eternal destiny. Billy Graham calls it "the hour of decision." I trust Billy Graham and his ministry, but more importantly I trust the Bible. If you are not already a believer, I pray that you, as a reader of *The Game of Life*, will make that decision. It's a matter of life or death. *The decision is yours to make.* Remember, if you don't choose life, or if you don't do anything and make no decision at all, you have automatically chosen death.

The Bible is clear on that point. You may have heard it said, "The Bible says it, I believe it, and that settles it!" Here's what God's Word says in John 3:17, 18, and 36:

> For God did not send His Son into the world to condemn the world, but that the world through Him might be saved. He who believes in Him is not condemned; but he who does not believe is condemned already, because he has not believed in the name of the only begotten Son of God.... He who believes in the Son has everlasting life; and he who does not believe in the Son shall not see life, but the wrath of God abides.

I don't believe it can be said any clearer, and that's why I am led to echo Paul's words as written to the Romans in Romans 1:16–17:

> For I am not ashamed of the gospel of Christ, for it is the power of God to salvation for everyone who believes, for the Jew first, and also for the Greek. For in it the righteousness of God is

revealed from faith to faith; as it is written, "The just shall live by faith."

I am not ashamed of presenting the gospel to you, the reader, and I pray you will not be ashamed or embarrassed to receive the gospel's free invitation to receive eternal life. You have nothing to lose, and life eternal to gain!

Dan and Margaret, 2004

Postlude

A Challenge to the Reader: A Penetrating Question

IF: You were to die tonight and you are thoroughly convinced you are going to heaven; and

IF: You are not a believer in Jesus Christ and have never accepted Him as Lord and Savior,

ASK YOURSELF THIS QUESTION: How do I know for sure I'm going to heaven? Or to put it another way, what is the basis for my belief in my certainty that I'm going to heaven?

ADDITIONAL QUESTION: Are you basing your certainty on your own efforts and all the good things you've done, and the fact that you've lived a good life, been at least reasonably successful, and never committed any "big" sins?

If there is any doubt whatsoever as to where you will spend eternity after you die, I would strongly encourage you to receive Jesus Christ right now and settle the issue.

Here's How You Can Receive Christ:

1. *Admit* you are a sinner.
2. *Be willing* to turn from your sins (repent).
3. *Believe* that Jesus died on the Cross and rose from the grave.
4. *Through prayer*, invite Jesus Christ to come in and control your life through the Holy Spirit (receive Him as Lord and Savior).

A Simple Prayer:

Dear Lord Jesus,

I know that I am a sinner, and I ask for Your forgiveness. I believe You died for my sins and rose from the dead. I now repent of my sins and invite You to come into my heart and live Your life through me. I want to trust and follow You as my Lord and Savior. In Jesus' name. Amen.

If You Sincerely Prayed That Prayer:

You have been born into God's family through the supernatural work of the Holy Spirit who dwells in every believer. This is called regeneration or the "new birth." The Bible says, "He who has the Son has life; he who does not have the Son of God does not have life" (1 John 5:12).

The Bottom Line

Whether we realize it or not, whether we believe it or not, whether we understand it or not, whether we think it's unfair or not, two things are for sure. They are inevitable:

1. The day is coming when all of us will die and leave this earthly existence to begin living throughout all eternity in either one of two places: In heaven with Christ Jesus or in hell without Him.
2. Before we leave our earthly existence, each one of us will either intentionally or unintentionally make a decision. The world offers us many choices; our eternal destiny, only two. The question of the ages for all of us is which one will we choose?

Will we intentionally choose to accept Christ and His free gift of eternal life?

OR